Nutrition Plan

Good Nutrition with Eating Clean Recipes and Intermittent Fasting

Robyn Olson and Kelley Glover

Copyright © 2013 Robyn Olson and Kelley Glover
All rights reserved.

Table of Contents

INTRODUCTION 1

SECTION 1: EATING CLEAN DIET 6
    5 Day Sample Meal Plan 12

EATING CLEAN DIET RECIPES 15

Eating Clean Diet Breakfast Recipes 15
    Apple Muffins 15
    Baked Oatmeal 17
    Blended Fruit Breakfast 19
    Breakfast Fruit Salad 20
    Coconut Oatmeal 22
    French Toast 24
    Fruit Salad with Yogurt Dressing 25
    Raisin Quinoa Pudding 27
    Strawberry, Banana, Oat Smoothie 29
    Toasted PB and B 30
    Turkey Sausage Casserole 31
    Vegetables Frittata 33
    Whole Grain Pancakes 35

Eating Clean Diet Appetizers, Snacks, and Dessert Recipes 37
    Baked Cinnamon Apple Toast 37
    Banana Oat Cookies 39
    Cinnamon Popcorn 40
    Deviled Eggs 41
    Guacamole 43
    Hummus Dip 44
    Peanut Butter Balls 45
    Sweet and Spicy Mango Salsa 47

Eating Clean Diet Side Dish Recipes 48
    Asparagus Mushroom Roast 48
    Authentic Pico de Gallo 50

Beans and Peppers ... 51
Cabbage Summer Casserole ... 52
Cauliflower and Greens ... 53
Fat Free Refried Beans ... 55
Herb Roasted Potatoes ... 57
Hot 'N Spicy Black Beans ... 58
Italian Sweet Potato Fries ... 59
Lemon Garlic Broccoli ... 60
Oven Roasted Vegetables ... 61
Potato Salad ... 63
Savory Quinoa ... 65
Spicy Pinto Beans ... 67
Spicy Roasted Baked Potatoes ... 69
Tangy Vegetable Salad ... 70

Eating Clean Main Dish Recipes ... 71
Baked Italian Crusted Cod ... 71
Balsamic Chicken and Rice. ... 73
Basic Spaghetti Sauce ... 75
Beefy Chili ... 77
Chicken Chili ... 79
Cod and Salsa ... 81
Fruit Salsa Salmon ... 82
Glazed Salmon ... 84
Grilled Turkey Breast ... 86
Honey Mustard Chicken ... 88
Italian Parmesan Eggplant ... 90
Mexican Chicken ... 92
Orange Lime Shrimp ... 93
Orange Roughy ... 95
Spicy Black Beans and Quinoa ... 96
Sweet and Tangy Tilapia ... 98
Tuna Salad ... 100
1Turkey Chili ... 101
Turkey Meatloaf ... 103

SECTION 2: INTERMITTENT FASTING DIET ... 105

Sample 5 Day Meal Plan ... 112

INTERMITTENT FASTING DIET RECIPES 114

Intermittent Fasting Diet Breakfast Recipes 114
- Breakfast Casserole 114
- Healthy Breakfast Burrito 116
- Mexican Style Eggs "Huevos Rancheros" 118
- Mexican Breakfast Casserole 120
- Savory Hash Browns 122
- Squash, Zucchini and Eggs 124
- Tomato Spinach Eggs 126
- Whole Grain Hot Cereal with Cherries 128
- Whole Wheat Pancakes with Apples 130
- Zucchini Frittata 132

Intermittent Fasting Diet Dinner Recipes 134
- Balsamic Turkey Meatloaf 134
- Buffalo Chicken with Slaw 136
- Edamame and Grilled Salmon 138
- Grilled Chicken Tostadas 140
- Italian Chicken 142
- Oriental Turkey Burgers 144
- Shepherd's Pie 147
- Shrimp Scampi 150
- Vegetable Pot Pie 152

Intermittent Fasting Diet Light Snack Recipes 154
- Apple and Turkey Ham Salad 154
- Baked Potatoes Twice 156
- Broccoli Cheese Soup 158
- Cauliflower Soup 160
- Greens with Baked Beans 162
- Maple Flavored Sweet Potato Fries 164
- Nutty Cucumber Mango Rice Salad 166
- Open Face Tomato and Mozzarella Herb Sandwich 168
- Orange Stir Fry Vegetables 170
- Parsley Mint Roasted Carrots 172
- Quinoa with Herbs 174
- Spicy Tomatoes and Green Beans 176
- Spinach Salad with Pomegranate Dressing 177

Introduction

The best way to enter into a healthy lifestyle is through a nutritious diet. By eating the right foods, you are giving your immune system a nice boost. The nutrients in the healthy foods go to work to strengthen the immune system, which then goes to work to help us overcome illnesses, and it also very much helps in the prevention of certain health conditions. Healthy whole foods are packed with high amounts of nutrients such as vitamins and minerals. Foods that contain anti-oxidants such as many vegetables and fruits are especially helpful in strengthening the immune system.

What if you are addicted to the wrong types of food? Junk food is void of any nutritional value or if it has any nutritional value at all, it is very little. Junk food is food that generally contains ingredients like sugar, trans fats, processed flours, and other foods that are worthless. Sugar is highly addictive and if you have a sugar addiction, you definitely have a junk food addiction. If you have to eat this type of food at least once a day or you get jittery, or a headache, or moody, then you have an addiction. Food addiction is as real and as bad an addiction as smoking cigarettes or drinking alcohol. If you truly want a healthy nutritious lifestyle, you must break the junk food habit.

To break the junk food habit you need to treat this as if you are breaking any bad habit. It takes about three weeks for the body to let go of a bad habit. While you are working on breaking this bad habit, you can begin your diet. Try the recipes from the eating clean diet. Replace the junk food with recipes from this book. Once you are weaned from the junk food you can go on the intermittent fasting diet and use it along with the eating clean diet successfully.

Start with eating junk food just twice a day for a week. Replace all other junk food times with healthy alternatives until you are fully weaned. The second week you can eat junk food just once a day. The third week, eat junk food once every other day. By the end of the third week, you should be weaned and should not have to suffer from the side effects like headaches and intense cravings. If you still feel you have an issue, rather than stopping the diet, try going two days between eating junk food for a week. And keep adding days until you are only eating it once a week.

By the time you are weaned from the junk food, you can go on the diets without risk of falling back into old eating habits because of the unpleasant withdrawals. This is the best way to start a new diet and a healthier lifestyle. Food is natures best way to help practice prevention and even treatment with many health conditions.

Any good nutrition plan should include drinking a lot of water. Water helps to cleanse the body of the toxins the junk food left behind. Water works with the healthy nutritious foods included in the eating clean and the intermittent fasting diet plans. A body needs a certain amount of water each day to function properly. You can derive some water from beverages other than water such as tea, coffee, and juice. You will receive some water from fruits and vegetables too. But you need to make sure you drink actual water each day. Calculate the amount of water by taking your weight in pounds and dividing that by two. That number will give you the amount in ounces you need. If you weigh 200 pounds, divided by two is 100 and so a 200-pound person will need to drink about 100 ounces of water a day to be at optimum health.

In addition to weaning from junk food and drinking plenty of water if you add exercise on top of it you will feel physically fit. It is a perfect addition to a healthy lifestyle. People who are in optimum health get plenty of exercise each week. Being physically active helps the body to feel better through the release of endorphins, a substance the brain releases when the body reaches a certain point during physical activity.

Physical activity need not be something that costs a lot of money or takes too much of your precious time. You can just do something every other day for a minimum of a half an hour at a time to make it work. You can walk or play sports or do anything that breaks a sweat. You can dance, run, swim, ride a bike, join a gym, or even something like cutting wood or working in a garden (if you are hoeing or digging). The point is if you so something that breaks a sweat you giving your body some well-deserved exercise.

Exercise will help to lose weight and boost your metabolism. This will give you more energy so you will feel like being physically active more. Exercise, drinking water, and the eating clean and intermittent fasting diets all work together to being a well-rounded healthy lifestyle.

Disclaimer

All the advice here is just for informational purposes only. This advice is not meant to diagnose or treat any health condition. You should always clarify with your health care provider any new diet or exercise you wish to pursue. As with anything in life, you will get out of it what you put in. If you wish to live a healthier lifestyle, you must do things to change your eating habits and add physical activity and then you shall see changes in your health turn around for the better. If you go on the diets and stick with them, you will have the results you are hoping to have. It is easy to quit and walk away. Stick with your determination to make a healthy lifestyle change. You have all you need to know right here. Clear it with your doctor and go for it.

Section 1: Eating Clean Diet

What is the eating clean diet?

The eating clean diet also called, clean eating diet or the eat clean diet, is a very simple and basic diet. It is the absence of anything chemical including processed flours and sugars, chemicals and preservatives, artificial dyes and flavors. It is food in its most natural state, the way it comes off the vine or plant or tree. It is food that you pick up at the produce section or from the freezer. You can find this food in the canned goods as well. Clean food diet is exactly what it sounds like.

Why Eat Clean Foods?

Eating foods on this diet puts you back to as close to nature as possible eating foods in their natural state without any processing or unnecessary ingredients. The body is able to assimilate foods better. It acts as a cleanse at first helping the body to detoxify from all the additives and preservatives. Natural foods help to keep the digestive system clean by acting as a natural scrubber as it goes through the tract.

Can you lose weight on this diet?

That is a big yes. Why? Because by not eating junk food the body has a chance to use all the nutrients that comes from clean foods to help boost the metabolism. This means that it digests the foods at the perfect time, pulling all the necessary nutrients out. Because there are no bad fats or sugars in natural foods the body does not hang on to them like it does when you consumer junk food. Because natural foods help the body to speed up the metabolism, you have more energy and when you have more energy you feel like getting up and moving around. Developing and maintaining a good exercise routine is vital in weight loss and very possible when consuming clean foods because you will have that extra energy.

Is the clean food diet healthy?

Yes. Consuming clean foods helps to boost the immune system. How? The best way to receive all the nutrients you need (nutrients as in vitamins, minerals, complex carbohydrates and more) is through the foods you eat. If you are eating whole healthy foods then your body is receiving all the nutrients it needs in order to keep you healthy.

The clean diet includes all the "super foods" like quinoa, spinach, and fruits and vegetables. These foods are high in nutrients and in particular in anti-oxidants. Anti-oxidants are vitamins and minerals that help to attack and get rid of free radicals in the body. Free radicals are substances that cause horrible diseases like cancer, heart disease and other debilitating diseases. If the body is able to fight free radicals it means the immune system is strong and healthy. And simply eating clean foods makes this happen.

Tips to make the eating clean diet work.

When you go grocery shopping of course you want to focus on all foods that are not labeled as "convenient food" or junk food. You will want to shop in the produce section (or your local farmer's market if available), the frozen foods section, and for canned goods.

Read labels. That is the only way you can be 100% sure you are purchasing truly clean foods. Read labels especially if you are purchasing prepackaged foods. Be very careful here. Even canned fruits and vegetables can contain unnecessary ingredients.

A general rule of thumb is if the ingredients are unrecognizable words, words with a lot of letters, words you cannot pronounce, they are probably preservatives and artificial colors and artificial flavors. Do not buy anything like this. Even if the package says it is all natural, always read the ingredients list. You can find some prepackaged foods that are all natural. But always read the labels.

If you cannot find certain natural foods at your regular grocery, you can always look at health food stores or whole food stores and find them. If all else fails seek out recipes to make your own from wholesome ingredients.

The recipes in this book calls for certain foods you can purchase and may consider prepackaged. Bread is one ingredient called for in several recipes. It is recommended to find a bread that has on the label that it contains no trans fats and no preservatives. Read the ingredients. You can find whole grain breads that are all natural.

Cooking spray is very handy to have. You can find sprays that are made from canola oil or olive oil. Avoid the ones that are "butter flavored" as they may contain artificial flavorings.

Yogurt is another food called for in some of the ingredients. You can find all natural plain yogurts in most grocery stores and certainly in whole foods or health food stores. Vanilla extract is another ingredient in some of the recipes. Be sure to get the 100% pure vanilla extract and not the imitation, which is full of chemicals.

Soy sauce comes in all natural forms, so read the labels and purchase the ones that contains all wholesome ingredients and avoid the others. Salsa is another ingredient you can purchase already made, and it is fairly easy to find jars of all natural salsas. If you cannot find them on the shelves, look in the produce section or the deli for store made, which are normally all natural. If you cannot find any that is all natural, salsa is easy to make. There are a few recipes in this book for some.

Vegetable stock is another ingredient (as well as chicken and sometimes you can use beef stock). Be careful when purchasing these, read the labels. Some are 100% all natural and organic and these are the best ones to purchase. You can also make your own when cooking vegetables, chicken, and beef.

Tomato sauces and pastes are called for in some of the ingredients. You can find all natural cans of these on most grocery shelves, just read the labels. If you cannot find them, make your own, it is not that hard.

Just Start!

Knowing what you can and cannot eat on this diet is easy, all you have to do is go grocery shopping and avoid the junk foods and the processed foods and you will do well. The good news is you do not have to order special meals, or join a club, or spend a lot of extra money on specialty diet foods to go on this diet. You just go shopping and buy whole healthy foods and you are on your way to healthy eating. Give your body a chance to be healthier and to feel better by eating the clean diet foods. This is a change in lifestyle and a change you will want to keep. Losing weight will come naturally if you are overweight. All you have to do is stay on the diet and not eat junk food. It helps to add exercise with it, because exercising will help to lose weight faster.

Lastly, always check with your health care provider before starting any new diet or exercise routine and make sure the foods you will be eating are good foods for you.

Disclaimer: the recipes within this book are tried and true recipes that have been around for years in some form or another. Enjoy trying the recipes, feel free to adjust to your own tastes, and needs.

5 Day Sample Meal Plan

Below is a sample meal plan that covers 5 days. For snacks and desserts it is good to include whole nuts and fruits. With the main dishes, include a green salad and steamed vegetables.

Day 1

Breakfast - Baked Oatmeal
Snack - Banana
Lunch - Spicy Black Beans and Quinoa
Snack - Sweet and Spicy Mango Salsa with whole grain chips
Supper - Baked Italian Crusted Cod
Dessert - Baked Cinnamon Apple Toast

Day 2

Breakfast - Turkey Sausage Casserole
Snack - Guacamole with whole grain chips
Lunch - Tuna Salad
Snack - Walnuts
Supper - Basic Spaghetti Sauce over spaghetti squash
Dessert - Peanut Butter Balls

Day 3

Breakfast - Strawberry Banana Oat Smoothie
Snack - Dried apricots
Lunch - Chicken Chili
Snack - Hummus Dip
Supper - Turkey Meatloaf with Spicy Roasted Baked Potatoes
Dessert - Cinnamon Popcorn

Day 4

Breakfast - Breakfast Fruit Salad Snack - Deviled Eggs
Lunch - Asparagus Mushroom Roast
Snack - Apple
Supper - Honey Mustard Chicken with Oven Roasted Vegetables
Dessert - Banana Oat Cookies

Day 5

Breakfast - Raisin Quinoa Pudding
Snack - Banana
Lunch - Tangy Vegetable Salad
Snack - Almonds
Supper - Orange Lime Shrimp with Cabbage Summer Casserole

Dessert - Fruit Salad with Yogurt Dressing (from the breakfast recipes)

Eating Clean Diet Recipes

Eating Clean Diet Breakfast Recipes

Apple Muffins

Here is a gluten free recipe using rice flour in a delicious muffin. Makes 6 muffins.

What You'll Need:

2 apples (Gala, peeled, cored, fine diced)
1 egg
1 cup of flour (white rice)
2/3 cup of yogurt (plain)
1/4 cup of oats (steel cut)
1/4 cup of cranberry juice
1 1/2 tablespoons of butter (melted)
1 tablespoon of flax seed
1 teaspoon of baking soda
1 teaspoon of cinnamon (ground)
1/2 teaspoon of nutmeg (ground)
1/2 teaspoon of arrowroot powder

How to Make It:

Prep: Preheat the oven to 350 degrees Fahrenheit. Spray a large 6 cup muffin pan with cooking spray. In a bowl mix the dry ingredients of 1 cup of flour (white rice), 1/4 cup of oats (steel cut), 1 tablespoon of flax seed, 1 teaspoon of baking soda, 1 teaspoon of cinnamon (ground), 1/2 teaspoon of nutmeg (ground), and the 1/2 teaspoon of arrowroot powder. In a separate bowl add the egg and beat with a whisk, then add the 2/3 cup of yogurt (plain), 1/4 cup of cranberry juice, and 1 1/2 tablespoons of butter (melted) and stir. Gradually add the dry ingredients and stir until just combined. Stir in the 2 apples (Gala, peeled, cored, fine diced). Pour evenly into the 6 large muffin cups. Bake until the muffins are golden brown, when a toothpick inserted in the middle of a muffin emerges clean, about half an hour. Cool for a couple of minutes and serve.

Baked Oatmeal

This delicious bowl of oatmeal has blueberries, applesauce, and cinnamon. Makes 8 servings.

What You'll Need:

3 cups of oats (rolled)
2 eggs
1 cups of blueberries (frozen)
1 cups of milk
1/2 cup of applesauce
1/2 cup of honey
1/8 cup of flax seed meal
1 1/2 tablespoons of wheat germ
1/2 tablespoon of baking powder
1/2 tablespoon of cinnamon (ground)
1 teaspoons of vanilla extract
1/4 teaspoons of salt
Butter
Milk

How to Make It:

Prep: Preheat the oven to 350 degrees Fahrenheit.

Mix the 3 cups of oats (rolled), 2 beaten eggs, 1 cups of

blueberries (frozen), 1 cups of milk, 1/2 cup of applesauce, 1/2 cup of honey, 1/8 cup of flax seed meal, 1 1/2 tablespoons of wheat germ, 1/2 tablespoon of baking powder, 1/2 tablespoon of cinnamon (ground), 1 teaspoons of vanilla extract, and 1/4 teaspoons of salt in a large bowl. Pour into a 9x9 inch baking dish or casserole dish. Bake for half an hour. Add extra butter and milk if desired when serving.

Blended Fruit Breakfast

This is a delicious and refreshing yet filling breakfast. Makes 2 servings.

What You'll Need:

6 apricots (dried, chopped)
1 cup of yogurt (plain)
1/2 cup of milk
1/2 cup of oats (rolled)
1/4 cup of oat bran
2 tablespoons of raisins
2 teaspoons of walnuts (chopped)
Ground cinnamon

How to Make It:

The night before: Combine the 6 apricots (dried, chopped), 1 cup of yogurt (plain), 1/2 cup of oats (rolled), 1/4 cup of oat bran, 2 tablespoons of raisins, and dashes of ground cinnamon. Cover and set in refrigerator. Next morning, divide between 2 bowls, pour 1/4 cup of milk and sprinkle 1 teaspoon of chopped walnuts over the top, serve.

Breakfast Fruit Salad

This is a refreshing breakfast, perfect for a hot summer morning, or as an anytime snack. Makes 10 servings.

What You'll Need:

3 kiwis (peeled, sliced)
3 bananas (peeled, sliced, ripe)
2 oranges (peeled, sectioned)
2 cups of pineapple (cubed)
2 cups of strawberries (hulled, sliced)
2 cups of blueberries
1 cup of grapes (seedless)
2/3 cups of orange juice
1/3 cup of lemon juice
1/3 cup of honey
1 teaspoon of vanilla extract
1/2 teaspoon of lemon zest
1/2 teaspoon of orange zest

How to Make It:

Pour the 2/3 cups of orange juice, 1/3 cup of honey, 1/3 cup of lemon juice, 1/2 teaspoon of lemon zest, and the 1/2 teaspoon of orange zest into a saucepan, stir and turn heat to medium high to bring to a boil. Turn to medium low, stir and cook for an additional 5 minutes. Stir in the 1 teaspoon of vanilla extract and set aside. In a large serving bowl (a large salad bowl works well) combine the 3 kiwis (peeled, sliced), 3 bananas (peeled, sliced, ripe), 2 oranges (peeled, sectioned), 2 cups of pineapple (cubed), 2 cups of strawberries (hulled, sliced), 2 cups of blueberries, and the 1 cup of grapes (seedless). Drizzle the cooked fruit juice over the top and toss. Place in the refrigerator for about 3 1/2 hours to chill before serving.

Coconut Oatmeal

Nothing quite satisfies hunger like a nice hot bowl of oatmeal first thing in the morning. Makes 6 servings.

What You'll Need:

3 1/2 cups of milk
2 cups of oats (rolled)
1 cup of yogurt (plain)
1/3 cup of raisins
1/3 cup of cranberries (dried)
1/3 cup of coconut (flaked)
1/3 cup of walnuts (chopped)
1/4 cup of maple syrup (pure)
3 tablespoons of honey
1/4 teaspoon of salt

How to Make It:

Add the 3 1/2 cups of milk and the 1/4 teaspoon of salt to a saucepan over high heat and carefully bring to a boil, watching and stirring constantly. Add the 2 cups of oats (rolled), 1/3 cup of raisins, 1/3 cup of cranberries (dried), and the 1/4 cup of maple syrup (pure), bring the mixture to a second boil, stirring constantly. Turn the heat down to medium and cook for another 5 minutes.

Add the 1/3 cup of coconut (flaked) and the 1/3 cup of walnuts (chopped), stir and cut the heat. Spoon into 6 bowls and divide the cup of plain yogurt and the 3 tablespoons of honey evenly among the bowls. Serve and enjoy.

French Toast

Everyone loves a batch of French toast for breakfast, a tasty sweet way to start the day. Makes 6 servings.

What You'll Need:

6 slices of whole grain bread
6 pats of butter
4 eggs
2/3 cup of milk
1 teaspoon of vanilla extract
1/2 teaspoon of cinnamon (ground)
Pure maple syrup

How to Make It:

Crack the 4 eggs into a shallow bowl and beat with a whisk. Add the 2/3 cup of milk, teaspoon of vanilla extract and the 1/2 teaspoon of ground cinnamon and stir to combine. Heat a skillet or griddle to medium high heat, spray with cooking spray. Dip each slice of bread in the egg mixture, coating all of it. Place on the hot skillet or griddle and cook until it turns a golden brown on the bottom, the flip and do the same. Repeat with each slice. Place a pat of butter on the hot toast. Drizzle with pure maple syrup and enjoy.

Fruit Salad with Yogurt Dressing

This is a refreshing breakfast with fresh fruit and a tangy yet sweet yogurt dressing. Makes 8 servings.

What You'll Need:

2 kiwis (peeled, chopped)
1 can of pineapples (crushed, 15 oz., in natural juices)
2 cups of yogurt (plain)
1 cup of grapes (red)
1 cup of strawberries (hulled, chopped)
1 cup of blueberries
1 cup of Granny Smith apples (cored, chopped)
1 cup of Fuji apples (cored, chopped)
2 tablespoons of lemon juice
2 tablespoons of honey

How to Make It:

Toss and combine the 2 kiwis (peeled, chopped), 1 can of pineapples (crushed, 15 oz., in natural juices), 1 cup of grapes (red), 1 cup of strawberries (hulled, chopped), 1 cup of blueberries, 1 cup of Granny Smith apples (cored, chopped), and the 1 cup of Fuji apples (cored, chopped) in a large bowl. In a small bowl add the 2 cups of plain yogurt, 2 tablespoons of lemon juice and 2 tablespoons of honey and stir with a whisk. Pour over the fruit and toss to coat. Serve and enjoy or store in the refrigerator.

Raisin Quinoa Pudding

This is a delightful breakfast with apple juice, raisins, and the super food quinoa. Makes 6 servings.

What You'll Need:

2 cups of water
2 cups of apple juice
1 cup of raisins
1 cup of quinoa
2 tablespoons of lemon juice
1 teaspoon of cinnamon (ground)
2 teaspoons of vanilla extract
Salt (if desired)

How to Make It:

Rinse the cup of quinoa in cheesecloth, squeezing out the excess. Add the quinoa to a saucepan and put the 2 cups of water over it. Turn to high heat and bring to a boil. Cover the saucepan and turn to low to simmer for about 15 minutes, until all the water is absorbed. Add the 2 cups of apple juice, 1 cup of raisins, 2 tablespoons of lemon juice, and 1 teaspoon of cinnamon (ground). Stir in salt if desired. Cook for 15 minutes on low, with lid on. Add the 2 teaspoons of vanilla extract at the last stir and serve.

Strawberry, Banana, Oat Smoothie

Sometimes you can simply drink your breakfast such as this delicious fruit smoothie. Makes 2 servings.

What You'll Need:

1 banana (peeled, chunked, frozen)
1 1/4 cup of strawberries (frozen)
1 cup of milk
1/2 cup of oats (rolled)
1/4 cup of ice
2 teaspoons of honey
1/2 teaspoon of vanilla extract

How to Make It:

Add the 1 banana (peeled, chunked, frozen), 1 1/4 cup of strawberries (frozen), 1 cup of milk, 1/2 cup of oats (rolled), 1/4 cup of ice, 2 teaspoons of honey, and the 1/2 teaspoon of vanilla extract into a blender or food processor and blend until smooth. Pour in a glass and enjoy.

Toasted PB and B

This is a toasted whole grain bread with natural peanut butter and bananas. Kids will love this breakfast. Makes 2 servings.

What You'll Need:

4 slices of whole grain bread
2 bananas
1/4 cup of peanut butter (natural creamy)
4 pats of butter

How to Make It:

Spread 1/8 cup of natural creamy peanut butter onto 2 slices of the whole grain bread. Peel and slice a banana on top of each peanut butter spread bread. Place another slice of whole grain bread on top the bananas. Add a pat of butter to a non-stick skillet over medium high heat and toast one side of one of the sandwiches. Repeat until both sides of each sandwich is toasted. Serve.

Turkey Sausage Casserole

This delicious casserole is wholesome and filling. Makes 8 servings.

What You'll Need:

1 pound of turkey sausage
6 slices of whole grain bread (toasted, cubed)
4 eggs
2 cups of milk
2 cups of cheddar cheese (mild, shredded)
1 teaspoon of mustard powder
Salt and pepper
Canola oil

How to Make It:

Prep: Preheat the oven to 350 degrees Fahrenheit. Spray a 9x13 inch baking dish with cooking spray.

Add a touch of canola oil to a skillet, then crumble and brown the pound of turkey sausage. Meanwhile, in a bowl, crack the 4 eggs and beat with a whisk. Combine with the 2 cups of milk, 1 teaspoon of mustard powder, and dashes of salt and pepper. Stir in the cooked turkey sausage, 6 slices of whole grain bread (toasted, cubed), and the 2 cups of cheddar cheese (mild, shredded). Pour into the prepared 9x13 inch baking dish and cover with foil and bake for 45 minutes. Turn the oven down to 325 degrees Fahrenheit, remove the foil cover, and bake for another half an hour, making sure the eggs are cooked. Let sit for 5 minutes before serving.

Vegetables Frittata

This is a delicious breakfast made with whole vegetables and fresh eggs. Makes 8 servings.

What You'll Need:

6 eggs
4 slices of whole grain bread (cubed)
2 packages of cream cheese (8 oz., diced, room temperature)
2 cups of cheddar cheese (sharp, shredded)
1 1/2 cups of zucchini (chopped)
1 1/2 cups of mushrooms (fresh chopped)
3/4 cup of onion (chopped)
3/4 cup of bell pepper (green chopped)
1/4 cup of half-and-half cream
3 tablespoons of canola oil
1/2 teaspoon of garlic (minced)
Salt and pepper

How to Make It:

Prep: Preheat the oven to 350 degrees Fahrenheit. Spray a 9x13 inch baking dish with cooking spray.

Pour the 3 tablespoons of canola oil into a skillet and

heat to medium high. Stir in the 1 1/2 cups of zucchini (chopped), 1 1/2 cups of mushrooms (fresh chopped), 3/4 cup of onion (chopped), 3/4 cup of bell pepper (green chopped), and the 1/2 teaspoon of garlic (minced) and sauté. Take off heat. In a bowl, crack the 6 eggs and beat with a whisk. Stir in the 1/4 cup of half-and-half cream. Then add the 4 slices of cubed whole grain bread, 2 8 oz. packages of diced cream cheese, 2 cups of cheddar cheese (sharp, shredded), and the cooked vegetables. Sprinkle dashes of salt and pepper and combine. Pour into the prepared 9x13 inch baking dish. Bake until the eggs set in the center, about 60 minutes. Allow to stand outside the oven for about 5 minutes before serving.

Whole Grain Pancakes

Drizzle your favorite pancake topping over these healthy whole grain pancakes for a delicious hot breakfast. Pure maple syrup recommended. Makes 4 servings.

What You'll Need:

2 eggs
2 cups of buttermilk
1 1/2 cups of flour (whole wheat pastry)
1/2 cup of wheat germ
1/4 cup of canola oil
2 teaspoons of baking soda
1/2 teaspoon of salt

How to Make It:

Mix the 1 1/2 cups of flour (whole wheat pastry), 1/2 cup of wheat germ, 1/2 teaspoons of baking soda, and 1/2 teaspoon of salt together. In a separate bowl, beat the 2 eggs with a whisk, then combine with the 2 cups of buttermilk, and 1/4 cup of canola oil. Add the dry ingredients and stir. Spray a griddle or large skillet with cooking spray and heat to medium high. Ladle a spoon of batter and cook until the edges dry and the center turns bubbly. Flip, repeat unto all the pancakes are made.

Eating Clean Diet Appetizers, Snacks, and Dessert Recipes

Baked Cinnamon Apple Toast

This is a quick and delicious snack, perfect for after school or as an impromptu dessert. Makes 4 servings.

What You'll Need:

1 apple (large, cored, sliced thin)
4 slices of whole grain bread
1 tablespoon of butter (room temperature, divided)
1 tablespoon of cinnamon (ground)
Honey

How to Make It:

Prep: Preheat the oven on broil (high).

Spread 1/4 tablespoon of butter onto one side of each slice of whole grain bread. Lay the bread on a baking sheet, butter side facing up. Evenly disperse the apple slices on top of each slice of bread. Sprinkle a few dashes of cinnamon on top of the apples. Drizzle a little honey on top of the cinnamon and apples. Place under the broiler until the edges of the bread turns to toast, a couple of minutes.

Banana Oat Cookies

These cookies are delicious with a nice cold glass of milk. Makes 36 cookies.

What You'll Need:

2 cups of bananas (ripe, chopped)
2 cups of oats (rolled)
1 cup of dates (pitted, chopped)
1/3 cup of canola oil
1 teaspoon of vanilla extract

How to Make It:

Prep: Preheat the oven to 350 degrees Fahrenheit.

Place the 2 cups of chopped bananas in a large bowl and mash with a potato masher. Add the 2 cups of oats (rolled), 1 cup of dates (pitted, chopped), 1/3 cup of canola oil, and 1 teaspoon of vanilla extract and mix. Set aside for about 15 minutes, and then drop by the spoonful's onto a baking sheet. Bake until cookies turn a golden brown about 20 minutes. Cool a few minutes on a wire rack before serving.

Cinnamon Popcorn

Healthy and wholesome, this snack will satisfy those in between meal hunger pangs. Makes 6 servings.

What You'll Need:

3/4 cup of popcorn kernels
3 tablespoons of olive oil
2 tablespoons of honey
Salt
Cinnamon (ground)

How to Make It:

Using a large pot with a lid, heat the 3 tablespoons of olive oil on high heat for 2 minutes. Pour in the 3/4 cup of popcorn kernels and replace the lid. Move the pot over the heat to prevent burning, shaking especially when the corn is popping. Pull from heat when the popping slows. Pour popped corn into a large bowl. Toss with the 2 tablespoons of honey, a couple dashes of salt and a dash or two of ground cinnamon.

Deviled Eggs

A classic recipe that always tastes great. Makes a dozen deviled eggs.

What You'll Need:

6 eggs
1 1/2 tablespoon of prepared mustard
1 1/2 tablespoon of mayonnaise
3/4 teaspoon of garlic salt
3/4 teaspoon of onion powder
Paprika
Water

How to Make It:

Put the 6 eggs into a medium saucepan and cover completely with cold water. Place saucepan on high heat and bring to a rapid boil for 10 minutes. Remove pan from heat and set on a cool burner for 5 minutes. Put pan in the sink and run cold water over the eggs. Let eggs sit in the cool water for a few minutes to cool. Remove the shells from the eggs and cut in half lengthwise. Carefully remove the yolks and place in a bowl. Add the 1 1/2 tablespoon of prepared mustard, 1 1/2 tablespoon of mayonnaise, 3/4 teaspoon of garlic salt, and 3/4 teaspoon of onion powder and mix well, incorporating the egg yolks into a creamy mixture. Spoon the egg yolk mixture back into the egg whites until it is all gone. Sprinkle with paprika. Store in the refrigerator for an hour before serving.

Guacamole

This is a great dip, great with Mexican dishes, and makes for wonderful snacks or appetizers. Makes 4 servings.

What You'll Need:

3 avocados (peeled, pitted, chopped)
1/4 cup of onions (diced)
3 tablespoons of cilantro (fresh chopped)
2 tablespoons of lime juice
1 teaspoon of garlic (minced)
Salt
Cayenne pepper

How to Make It:

Place the 3 avocados (peeled, pitted, chopped) in a blender or food processor and blend until smooth. Add in the 2 tablespoons of lime juice and several dashes of salt. Transfer to a bowl and combine with the 1/4 cup of onions (diced), 3 tablespoons of cilantro (fresh chopped) 1 teaspoon of garlic (minced), and a dash or two of the cayenne pepper. Refrigerate for half an hour before serving.

Hummus Dip

Enjoy a nutritious snack with pita chips or whole grain crackers. Makes 4 servings.

What You'll Need:

1 can of garbanzo beans (15 oz., drained but keep the liquid)
1 tablespoon of olive oil
2 teaspoons of cumin (ground)
1/2 teaspoon of garlic (minced)
Salt

How to Make It:

Add the 1 can of drained garbanzo beans, 1 tablespoon of olive oil, 2 teaspoons of cumin (ground), 1/2 teaspoon of garlic (minced), and dashes of salt into a food processor or blender and combine until smooth. Add the extra can liquid if needed.

Peanut Butter Balls

A delicious treat that both kids and adults love. If you are inclined, add a few semi-sweet chocolate chips to the mix. Makes 2 dozen.

What You'll Need:

1/2 cup of peanut butter (natural creamy)
1/3 cup of oats (rolled)
1/4 cup of apple juice (from the frozen can of concentrate, thawed)
1/4 cup of coconut (flakes)
1/4 cup of powdered milk
1/4 cup of wheat germ
1/2 teaspoon of cinnamon (ground)
Peanuts (finely chopped)

How to Make Them:

In a large bowl combine 1/2 cup of peanut butter (natural crunchy), 1/3 cup of oats (rolled), 1/4 cup of apple juice (from the frozen can of concentrate, thawed), 1/4 cup of coconut (flakes), 1/4 cup of powdered milk, 1/4 cup of wheat germ, and 1/2 teaspoon of cinnamon (ground). Roll into 2 dozen balls, then roll through the fine chopped peanuts.) Place in a container to store in the refrigerator.

Sweet and Spicy Mango Salsa

This is a different twist with a salsa, fruity yet hot and spicy. Makes 5 cups.

What You'll Need:

2 cups of Roma tomatoes (diced)
1 1/2 cups of mango (dried)
1/2 cup of cilantro (fresh chopped)
1/2 cup of onion (diced)
2 tablespoons of lime juice
1 tablespoon of apple cider vinegar
1 tablespoon of honey
1 teaspoon of garlic (minced)
Salt and pepper

How to Make It:

Combine the 2 cups of Roma tomatoes (diced), 1 1/2 cups of mango (dried), 1/2 cup of cilantro (fresh chopped), 1/2 cup of onion (diced), 2 tablespoons of lime juice, 1 tablespoon of apple cider vinegar, 1 tablespoon of honey, 1 teaspoon of garlic (minced), and dashes of salt and pepper in a large bowl. Cover and refrigerate for 60 minutes.

Eating Clean Diet Side Dish Recipes

Asparagus Mushroom Roast

You have a hit when you combine delicious asparagus with tasty mushrooms. Makes 6 servings.

What You'll Need:

.5 pound of mushrooms (fresh, quartered)
1 bunch of asparagus (trimmed)
2 sprigs of rosemary (minced)
2 teaspoons of olive oil
Salt and pepper

How to Make It:

Prep: Preheat oven to 450 degrees Fahrenheit. Line a baking sheet with foil and spray it with cooking spray.

Toss together the .5 pound of mushrooms (fresh, quartered), 1 bunch of asparagus (trimmed), 2 sprigs of rosemary (minced), 2 teaspoons of olive oil, and dashes of salt and pepper. Spread on the prepared baking sheet and bake for 15 minutes, until the asparagus and mushrooms are tender.

Authentic Pico de Gallo

When eating south-of-the-border cuisine you need a delicious side dish of pico de gallo. Makes 4 servings.

What You'll Need:

2 sprigs of cilantro (chopped fine)
1 scallion (chopped fine)
1 tomato (diced)
1/2 jalapeno pepper (seeded, chopped)
1/2 cup of onions (chopped)
1/2 teaspoon of garlic (powder)
Salt and pepper

How to Make It:

Combine the 2 sprigs of cilantro (chopped fine), 1 scallion (chopped fine), 1 tomato (diced), 1/2 jalapeno pepper (seeded, chopped), 1/2 cup of onions (chopped), 1/2 teaspoon of garlic (powder), and dashes of salt and pepper in a bowl. Set in the refrigerator for half an hour at least before serving.

Beans and Peppers

This is a tasty dish made with great northern beans and banana peppers. Makes 4 servings.

What You'll Need:

1 can of great northern beans (drained)
2 banana peppers (chopped)
1/4 cup of onion (chopped)
1 teaspoon of olive oil
Oregano
Cayenne pepper
Salt and pepper

How to Make It:

Add the teaspoon of olive oil to a skillet heated to medium. Add the 2 banana peppers (chopped) and the 1/4 cup of onion (chopped) and sauté. Stir in the 1 can of great northern beans (drained), and dashes of oregano, cayenne pepper, salt and pepper. Keep on heat until heated through.

Cabbage Summer Casserole

This is a delightful dish with zucchini, squash and cabbage, you cannot go wrong with this. Makes 4 servings.

What You'll Need:

1 zucchini (sliced)
1 squash (yellow, sliced)
4 cups of cabbage (sliced)
2 cups of chicken stock
3/4 cup of onions (chopped)
Salt and pepper

How to Make It:

Combine the 1 zucchini (sliced), 1 squash (yellow, sliced), 4 cups of cabbage (sliced), 2 cups of chicken stock, 3/4 cup of onions (chopped), and dashes of salt and pepper in a large sauce pan and turn heat to high. Bring liquid to a boil, reduce heat to medium and continue cooking for 30 minutes.

Cauliflower and Greens

This is a delicious side dish made of cauliflower and kale with a refreshing lemon dressing. Makes 4 servings.

What You'll Need:

1 head of cauliflower (chopped bite-sized chunks)
1 bunch of kale (chopped)
4 cups of water
3 tablespoons of currants (dried)
2 tablespoons of olive oil (extra virgin)
1 tablespoon of Dijon mustard
1 tablespoon of lemon juice
2 teaspoons of lemon zest
Salt and pepper

How to Make It:

Combine the 1 tablespoon of Dijon mustard, 1 tablespoon of lemon juice, and the 2 teaspoons of lemon zest using a whisk. Add the 2 tablespoons of olive oil (extra virgin), whisk well. Stir in the 3 tablespoons of currants (dried).

Meanwhile, add the 4 cups of water to a steamer pot and turn to high to bring to a boil. Place the head of chopped bite-sized cauliflower chunks into the steamer and steam until tender, about 4 minutes. Toss the cauliflower in the bowl of dressing. Remove the steamer pan and place the bunch of chopped kale into the boiling water and continuing boiling for around 3 minutes. Drain the water and add the kale to the cauliflower, and toss to coat. Add dashes of salt and pepper and serve.

Fat Free Refried Beans

Refried beans are the perfect addition to a south-of-the-border meal. Makes 8 servings.

What You'll Need:

4 1/2 cups of water
1 1/2 cups of pinto beans (dried, sorted, rinsed)
1/4 cup of onions (chopped)
1/4 of a jalapeno pepper (seeded, finely chopped)
1 tablespoon of garlic (minced)
2 1/2 teaspoons of salt
1 teaspoon of black pepper
Pinch of cumin (ground)

How to Make It:

Add the 1 1/2 cups of pinto beans (dried, sorted, rinsed), 1/4 cup of onions (chopped), 1/4 of a jalapeno pepper (seeded, finely chopped), 1 tablespoon of garlic (minced), 2 1/2 teaspoons of salt, 1 teaspoon of black pepper, and a pinch of cumin (ground) in a slow cooker. Pour the 4 1/2 cups of water over the top. Cook on high for 8 hours, check often, and if needed add more water to make sure all the ingredients are covered. When the beans are good and tender, remove them from the liquid into a large bowl and mash them with a potato masher, adding extra liquid as needed to reach the right consistency.

Herb Roasted Potatoes

Healthier than fried potatoes, these offers a spicy taste with each bite. Makes 4 servings.

What You'll Need:

4 potatoes (large, scrubbed, peeled, cubed into bite-size)
1 tablespoon of basil (fresh chopped)
1 tablespoon of garlic (minced)
1 tablespoon of olive oil
1 tablespoon of parsley (fresh chopped)
1 tablespoon of rosemary (fresh chopped)
1/2 teaspoon of salt

How to Make It:

Prep: Preheat the oven to 475 degrees Fahrenheit. Line a baking sheet with foil.

Add the 1 tablespoon of basil (fresh chopped), 1 tablespoon of garlic (minced), 1 tablespoon of olive oil, 1 tablespoon of parsley (fresh chopped), 1 tablespoon of rosemary (fresh chopped), and 1/2 teaspoon of salt in a bowl and mix with a whisk. Add the 4 peeled and cubed potatoes and toss to coat all. Bake for 30 minutes, turning every 10 minutes. Serve immediately.

Hot 'N Spicy Black Beans

Beans make a great side dish and these give a little added flavor kick. Makes 4 servings.

What You'll Need:

1 can of black beans (15 oz., undrained)
1/2 cup of onions (chopped)
1 tablespoon of cilantro (fresh chopped)
1/2 teaspoon of garlic (minced)
1/4 teaspoon of cayenne pepper
Salt

How to Make It:

Add the 1 can of black beans (15 oz., undrained), 1/2 cup of onions (chopped), and 1/2 teaspoon of garlic (minced), to a saucepan, turn the heat to high and bring to a boil, turn to medium low and stir in the 1 tablespoon of cilantro (fresh chopped), 1/4 teaspoon of cayenne pepper, and dashes of salt. Serve immediately.

Italian Sweet Potato Fries

This is a healthier version of the French fry. Makes 4 servings.

What You'll Need:

4 sweet potatoes (peeled, cut into French fries)
2 tablespoons of olive oil
2 teaspoons of Italian seasoning
1/2 teaspoon of lemon pepper
Salt and pepper
Water

How to Make It:

Prep: Preheat the oven to 400 degrees Fahrenheit.

Place a saucepan on the stove and add the 4 French fry cut sweet potatoes, cover with water and turn to high heat. Boil for 5 minutes. Drain water and toss in the 2 tablespoons of olive oil, 2 teaspoons of Italian seasoning, 1/2 teaspoon of lemon pepper, and dashes of Salt and pepper. Spread on a baking sheet and bake for 15 minutes, flip and bake for another 15 minutes.

Lemon Garlic Broccoli

This is a roasted broccoli with lemon and garlic flavors added for a delicious side dish. Makes 6 servings.

What You'll Need:

2 broccoli heads (just the florets)
2 teaspoons of olive oil (extra virgin)
1/2 teaspoon of garlic (minced)
1/2 teaspoon of lemon juice
Salt and pepper

How to Make It:

Prep: Preheat the oven to 400 degrees Fahrenheit.

Add the florets from the 2 broccoli heads to a large bowl and toss with the 2 teaspoons of olive oil (extra virgin), 1/2 teaspoon of garlic (minced), and dashes of salt and pepper. Place in a single layer on a foil-lined baking sheet and bake until tender for about 17 minutes. Place in a serving bowl and toss with the 1/2 teaspoon of lemon juice. Serve immediately.

Oven Roasted Vegetables

Here is a quick and easy way to get in a good serving of savory vegetables. Makes 6 servings.

What You'll Need:

4 potatoes (scrubbed, sliced into bite size)
1 package of frozen vegetables (10 oz. mixed)
1/2 cup of onions (chopped)
5 tablespoons of butter (divided into 10 small pats)
1 tablespoon of Italian seasoning
1 teaspoon of garlic (minced)
Salt and pepper

How to Make It:

Prep: Heat oven to 350 degrees Fahrenheit. Place 2 sheets of heavy duty foil side by side on a baking sheet, have 2 more sheets for the top. Lightly spray the foil with cooking spray on one side.

In a large bowl, combine by tossing together the 4 potatoes (scrubbed, sliced into bite size), 1 package of frozen vegetables (10 oz. mixed), 1/2 cup of onions (chopped), 1 tablespoon of Italian seasoning, 1 teaspoon of garlic (minced), and dashes of salt and pepper. Spoon equally on the center of each sheet of foil on the baking sheet. Place 5 pats of butter on top of each vegetable pile. Bring the bottom foil up to form a bowl, and place a sheet of foil on top and seal the edges, to make 2 "packets" of foil with the veggies enclosed. Bake in the oven for 15 minutes, check to make sure the potatoes are tender. Keep baking and checking every 5 minutes until the potatoes are tender enough to eat.

Potato Salad

Potato salad is a great side dish that goes with so many different main dishes. Makes 6 servings.

What You'll Need:

5 potatoes (Yukon gold)
1 cucumber (chopped, English)
2 1/2 cups of celery (chopped)
3/4 cup of onions (chopped)
3/4 cup of olives (green with pimentos, chopped)
1/2 cup of balsamic vinegar
1/4 cup of olive oil
1/4 teaspoon of garlic powder
Salt and pepper

How to Make It:

Scrub the 5 Yukon gold potatoes and place, whole, in a large saucepan. Cover the potatoes with water and turn the heat to high to bring to a boil. Turn the heat down to medium low and cook the potatoes for another 15 minutes. Drain the water and allow to cool for a few minutes. Then cut into bite sized chunks, peels and all. In a bowl, combine the cooked potatoes with the 1 cucumber (chopped, English), 2 1/2 cups of celery (chopped), 3/4 cup of onions (chopped), and the 3/4 cup of olives (green with pimentos, chopped). In a small bowl, combine the 1/2 cup of balsamic vinegar, 1/4 cup of olive oil, 1/4 teaspoon of garlic powder, and dashes of salt and pepper with a whisk. Drizzle over the potato salad and toss to coat. Refrigerate before serving. Add more salt and pepper if desired, toss again before serving.

Savory Quinoa

Quinoa is a super food packed with nutrition. It is delicious and makes a great side dish. Makes 4 servings.

What You'll Need:

2 cups of vegetable stock
1 cup of quinoa (uncooked)
1/2 cup of onions (chopped)
2 tablespoons of parsley (fresh chopped)
1 tablespoon of butter
1/2 tablespoon of thyme (fresh chopped)
2 teaspoons of garlic (minced)
Salt
Lemon juice

How to Make It:

Place the tablespoon of butter in a saucepan and turn to medium heat. Stir in the cup of uncooked quinoa, and brown for five minutes, stirring often. Add the 2 cups of vegetable stock and turn heat to high to bring to a boil. Reduce heat to low and simmer for 15 minutes with a lid to cover. Check to see if the quinoa is tender, if not, keep cooking until it becomes tender. Add the cooked quinoa in a bowl and toss in the 1/2 cup of onions (chopped), 2 tablespoons of parsley (fresh chopped), 1 tablespoon of butter, 1/2 tablespoon of thyme (fresh chopped), 2 teaspoons of garlic (minced), and dashes of salt and lemon juice. Serve immediately.

Spicy Pinto Beans

Take your average pot of pinto beans and turn up the heat, way up! Makes 8 servings.

What You'll Need:

1 lb. of pinto beans (dried)
1 jalapeno (fine chopped)
3 2/3 cup of chicken stock
3/4 cup of onions (chopped)
1/2 cup of green salsa
1 teaspoon of cumin (ground)
1 teaspoon of garlic (minced)
Salt and pepper
Water

How to Make It:

Prep: Sort, rinse, and soak the beans overnight.

Combine the 1 lb. of pinto beans (dried), 1 jalapeno (fine chopped), 3 2/3 cup of chicken stock, 3/4 cup of onions (chopped), 1/2 cup of green salsa, 1 teaspoon of cumin (ground), 1 teaspoon of garlic (minced), and dashes of salt and pepper in a large pan on the stove. Turn to high heat and bring to a boil. Turn to medium low and cook until the beans are tender, about 2 hours. Add more water if needed.

Spicy Roasted Baked Potatoes

This is a delicious combination of spicy and sweet. Makes 4 servings.

What You'll Need:

3 sweet potatoes (large, washed, peeled, and cut into chunks)
2 tablespoons of olive oil
Dried oregano
Salt and Pepper

How to Make It:

Prep: Preheat the oven to 350 degrees Fahrenheit. Line a baking sheet with foil and spray it with cooking spray.

Place the sweet potatoes in a large bowl, toss in 2 tablespoons of olive oil. Sprinkle the dried oregano, salt, and pepper and toss again so that all pieces are coated with oil and seasonings. Spread the chunks out onto a baking sheet and bake for at least an hour, until they are tender. Serve immediately.

Tangy Vegetable Salad

This is a delicious side dish or a night light lunch. Makes 8 servings.

What You'll Need:

3 cans of corn (11 oz., whole kernel)
4 scallions (chopped)
2 tomatoes (diced)
1 bunch of cilantro (fresh chopped)
3/4 cup of onions (thin sliced)
1/3 cup of rice vinegar
Salt

How to Make It:

Combine the 3 cans of corn (11 oz., whole kernel), 4 scallions (chopped), 2 tomatoes (diced), 1 bunch of cilantro (fresh chopped), and 3/4 cup of onions (thin sliced), tossing. Drizzle and toss the 1/3 cup of rice vinegar and a couple dashes of salt. Refrigerate for about 30 to 45 minutes. Toss again prior to serving.

Eating Clean Main Dish Recipes

Baked Italian Crusted Cod

Cod is nutritious and a good way to get in the weekly fish you should be eating. The cod has an Italian crust that tastes fried even though it was baked. Makes 4 servings.

What You'll Need:

4 cod fillets
1/4 cup of bread crumbs (from whole grain bread)
1 egg white
2 tablespoons of Parmesan cheese (grated)
1 tablespoon of cornmeal
1 teaspoon of olive oil
1/2 teaspoon of Italian seasoning
1/2 teaspoon of garlic (minced)
1/8 teaspoon of black pepper (ground)

How to Make It:

Prep: Preheat the oven to 450 degrees Fahrenheit.

Combine the 1/4 cup of bread crumbs (from whole grain bread), 2 tablespoons of Parmesan cheese (grated), 1 tablespoon of cornmeal, 1 teaspoon of olive oil, 1/2 teaspoon of Italian seasoning, 1/2 teaspoon of garlic (minced), and 1/8 teaspoon of black pepper (ground) in a bowl. Spray a boiler pan with cooking spray. Place the cod on the boiler pan. Beat the egg white slightly, and then brush onto the tops of the cod fillets. Evenly divide the breadcrumb mixture onto the tops of the cod. Bake until the fish is done, when it flakes apart, about 11 minutes.

Balsamic Chicken and Rice.

This savory chicken dish is an excellent companion with a side dish of rice. Makes 6 servings.

What You'll Need:

6 chicken breast halves (boneless, skinless)
1 can of tomatoes (14.5 oz., diced)
1/2 cup of onion (thin sliced)
1/2 cup of balsamic vinegar
2 tablespoons of olive oil
1 teaspoon of garlic salt
1 teaspoon of basil (dried)
1 teaspoon of oregano (dried)
1 teaspoon of rosemary (dried)
1/2 teaspoon of thyme (dried)
Black pepper
Rice (cooked, enough for 6 servings)

How to Make It:

Sprinkle the teaspoon of garlic salt and a couple of dashes of black pepper on the 6 boneless, skinless chicken breast halves. Add the 2 tablespoons of olive oil to a skillet and heat to medium high and cooked the chicken breasts and sauté the 1/2 cup of thin sliced onion. Add the can of 14.5 oz. can of diced tomatoes and the 1/2 cup of balsamic vinegar over the chicken. Stir in the 1 teaspoon of basil (dried), 1 teaspoon of oregano (dried), 1 teaspoon of rosemary (dried), and 1/2 teaspoon of thyme (dried). Cooking for about 15 minutes, until the chicken turns solid white. Serve a breast half over a spoon of cooked rice.

Basic Spaghetti Sauce

This is a savory, delicious sauce that tastes great over chicken, homemade pasta, eggplants, vegetables, or wherever spaghetti sauce is used. Makes 8 servings.

What You'll Need:

2 cans of tomato sauce (15 oz. each)
1 can of tomatoes (14.5 oz., stewed)
1 can of tomato paste (6 oz.)
4 mushrooms (fresh, sliced)
1 bell pepper (green ,chopped)
1/2 cup of onion (chopped)
1 tablespoon of olive oil
1 1/2 teaspoons of garlic (minced)
1/4 teaspoon of basil (dried)
1/4 teaspoon of oregano (dried)
Black pepper

How to Make It:

Add the tablespoon of olive oil to a skillet and turn to medium heat. Sauté the 1 bell pepper (green ,chopped), 1/2 cup of onion (chopped), and the 1 1/2 teaspoons of garlic (minced). Stir in the 1/4 teaspoon of basil (dried), 1/4 teaspoon of oregano (dried), and dashes of black pepper. Add the 14.5 oz. can of stewed tomatoes and cook until the sauce thickens. Add the 2 15 oz. cans of tomato sauce and the 6 oz. can of tomato paste. Turn heat to low, stir and simmer for 15 minutes.

Beefy Chili

This is a tried and true traditional chili recipe. Makes 8 servings.

What You'll Need:

1 pound of ground beef (lean)
2 cans of tomato puree (10.75 oz.)
2 cans of kidney beans (15 oz. each, 1 undrained and 1 drained)
1 can of cannellini beans (15 oz., undrained)
3/4 cup of onions (diced)
3/4 cup of celery (dice)
3/4 cup of bell pepper (green, diced)
1/2 tablespoon of chili powder
1 teaspoon of garlic (minced)
3/4 teaspoon of basil (dried)
3/4 teaspoon of oregano (dried)
1/2 teaspoon of parsley (dried)
Couple shakes of hot pepper sauce
Salt and pepper

How to Make It:

Cook the pound of lean ground beef over medium high heat in a skillet. Drain off grease. Add the cooked beef to a slow cooker followed by 2 cans of tomato puree (10.75 oz.), 2 cans of kidney beans (15 oz. each, 1 undrained and 1 drained), 1 can of cannellini beans (15 oz., undrained), 3/4 cup of onions (diced), 3/4 cup of celery (dice), 3/4 cup of bell pepper (green, diced), 1/2 tablespoon of chili powder, 1 teaspoon of garlic (minced), 3/4 teaspoon of basil (dried), 3/4 teaspoon of oregano (dried), 1/2 teaspoon of parsley (dried), a couple shakes of hot pepper sauce, and dashes of salt and pepper. Stir, cover, and cook on low for eight hours or on high for four hours.

Chicken Chili

This is a bowl of delicious spicy chicken chili, the perfect comfort food. Makes 4 servings.

What You'll Need:

4 chicken breasts (halves, boneless, skinless, cubed)
1 can of cannellini beans (15 oz., drained, rinsed)
1 can of green chilies (4 oz., diced)
2 green onions (chopped)
1 1/4 cups of chicken stock
1/2 cup of Monterey Jack cheese (shredded)
1/2 cup of onion (chopped)
1 tablespoon of olive oil
1 teaspoon of garlic powder
1 teaspoon of cumin (ground)
1/2 teaspoon of cilantro (dried)
1/2 teaspoon of oregano (dried)
1/8 teaspoon of cayenne pepper

How to Make It:

Add the tablespoon of olive oil to a large size saucepan and turn to medium high heat. Add the 4 chicken breasts (halves, boneless, skinless, cubed) and the 1/2 cup of chopped onions and cook for 5 minutes, while stirring. Pour in the 1 1/4 cups of chicken stock and add the 1 can of green chilies (4 oz., diced), 1 teaspoon of garlic powder, 1 teaspoon of cumin (ground), 1/2 teaspoon of cilantro (dried), 1/2 teaspoon of oregano (dried), and the 1/8 teaspoon of cayenne pepper. Turn the heat to low and cook for 15 minutes. Add the 1 can of cannellini beans (15 oz., drained, rinsed) and cook until the chicken is well done and white about another five minutes. Ladle into bowls and divide the 2 chopped green onions and the 1/2 cup of shredded Monterey Jack cheese on top.

Cod and Salsa

This is a delicious spicy cod, if you want it hot use a hotter salsa. Makes 4 servings.

What You'll Need:

1.5 pounds of cod fillets (rinse and pat dry)
2 cups of salsa
2 tablespoons of parsley (fresh chopped)
Lemon juice
Salt and pepper
Rice (cooked, 4 servings)

How to Make It:

Prep: Preheat the oven to 350 degrees Fahrenheit. Line a baking dish with foil and lightly spray with cooking spray.

Sprinkle the 2 tablespoons of fresh chopped parsley, lemon juice, and dashes of salt and pepper over the cod. Bake until flaky for about half an hour. Serve each serving over a serving of cooked rice.

Fruit Salsa Salmon

This is a deliciously sweet and spicy salmon dish, perfect over a bed of rice. Makes 4 servings.

What You'll Need:

1 pound of salmon steaks
Rice (cooked, enough for 4 servings)
2 jalapeno peppers (diced)
1 tomato (diced)
1 lemon (sliced)
1/2 cup of pineapple juice
1/3 cup of water
1/4 cup of bell pepper (red, diced)
1/4 cup of bell pepper (yellow, diced)
1/4 cup of pineapple (fresh diced)
1/4 cup of onion (minced)
2 tablespoons of lemon juice
1 tablespoon of rosemary (fresh chopped)
1 1/2 teaspoons of garlic (minced)
Salt and pepper

How to Make It:

Prep: Preheat the oven to 350 degrees Fahrenheit.

Place the salmon steaks in a shallow baking pan, sprinkle the 2 tablespoons of lemon juice over the top. Sprinkle with the 1 tablespoon of rosemary (fresh chopped) and dashes of salt and pepper. Cover with slices of the lemon. Add the 1/3 cup of water to the pan. Bake for 40 minutes, after the water evaporates and the fish is flakey it is done. In a bowl, make the fruit salsa by combining the 2 jalapeno peppers (diced), 1 tomato (diced), 1/2 cup of pineapple juice, 1/3 cup of water, 1/4 cup of bell pepper (red, diced), 1/4 cup of bell pepper (yellow, diced), 1/4 cup of pineapple (fresh diced), 1/4 cup of onion (minced), 1 tablespoon of rosemary (fresh chopped), and 1 1/2 teaspoons of garlic (minced). Divide the salmon steaks into 4 servings. Add a serving of rice on the plate, top with a salmon steak, and then 1/4 of the fruit salsa. Serve immediately.

Glazed Salmon

Here is a delicious spicy hot and sweet glazed salmon. Makes 4 servings.

What You'll Need:

1 salmon filet (.75 pound, skinless)
1 1/2 cups of apricot nectar
1/3 cup of apricots (chopped, dried)
2 tablespoons of honey
2 tablespoons of soy sauce
1 tablespoon of ginger (fresh grated)
1 teaspoon of garlic (minced)
1/4 teaspoon of cinnamon (ground)
1/8 teaspoon of cayenne pepper

How to Make It:

Prep: Preheat the boiler on high. Spray the boiler pan with cooking spray.

Combine the 1 1/2 cups of apricot nectar, 1/3 cup of apricots (chopped, dried), 2 tablespoons of honey, 2 tablespoons of soy sauce, 1 tablespoon of ginger (fresh grated), 1 teaspoon of garlic (minced), 1/4 teaspoon of cinnamon (ground), and the 1/8 teaspoon of cayenne pepper in a saucepan over medium heat, stirring often until it comes to a boil. Turn to medium low and cook for 20 minutes. Stir often to prevent sticking and burning. Pull out 1/4 cup of liquid and set aside. Put the salmon filet on the prepared boiler pan. Brush with the glaze in the saucepan. Place under the boiler for 8 minutes. Then baste ever minute for 4 more minutes. Remove from oven, serve with the reserved glaze.

Grilled Turkey Breast

This is a delicious dish of seasoned savory turkey breast. Makes about 10 servings.

What You'll Need:

2 turkey breast (boneless, halves)
1/4 cup of canola oil
1/4 cup of soy sauce
6 cloves (whole)
2 tablespoons of lemon juice
1 tablespoon of honey
1 tablespoon of basil (fresh chopped)
1 teaspoon of garlic (minced)
1/2 teaspoon of black pepper (ground)

How to Make It:

First, combine the 1 tablespoon of basil (fresh chopped), 1 teaspoon of garlic (minced), and the 1/2 teaspoon of black pepper (ground). This is the rub, wash and pat dry the boneless turkey breast halves, then rub into each one. In a separate bowl, combine the 1/4 cup of canola oil, 1/4 cup of soy sauce, 2 tablespoons of lemon juice, and the 1 tablespoon of honey. Coat the turkey breast halves in the marinade. Arrange them in a baking dish and place the 6 cloves all around the breasts. Seal with foil and refrigerate for four hours. Turn the grill to high. Spray the grate with cooking spray. Grill the turkey breasts on the hot grill, lid closed, for 30 minutes, flipping half way through. Check to make sure the internal temperature reaches 170 degrees Fahrenheit.

Honey Mustard Chicken

This is recipe is a favorite for young and old alike. Makes 6 servings.

What You'll Need:

6 chicken breast halves (boneless, skinless)
1/2 cup of honey
1/2 cup of yellow prepared mustard
1 teaspoon of basil (dried)
1 teaspoon of paprika
1/2 teaspoon of parsley (dried)
Salt and pepper

How to Make It:

Prep: Preheat the oven to 350 degrees Fahrenheit. Line a 9x13 inch baking dish with foil and lightly spray with cooking spray.

Rinse and dry the 6 boneless, skinless chicken breast halves and sprinkle with dash of salt and pepper. Lay the chicken in the prepared baking dish. Make the sauce by combining the 1/2 cup of honey, 1/2 cup of yellow prepared mustard, 1 teaspoon of basil (dried), 1 teaspoon of paprika, and 1/2 teaspoon of parsley (dried) in a bowl with a whisk. Brush on all sides of the seasoned chicken breasts. Bake in the hot oven for 15 minutes. Turn the oven off and let sit in the cooling oven for 10 minutes before serving.

Italian Parmesan Eggplant

This delicious dish uses the Basic Spaghetti Sauce recipe as well, making a delightful Italian dish. Makes 8 servings.

What You'll Need:

12 slices of whole grain bread
3 eggplants (peeled, sliced thin)
2 eggs
6 cups of spaghetti sauce (use the Basic Spaghetti Sauce recipe)
4 cups of mozzarella cheese (shredded, divided)
1/2 cup of Parmesan cheese (grated, divided)
1/2 teaspoon of basil (dried)
Italian seasoning
Olive oil (to drizzle)

How to Make It:

First, make the breadcrumbs. Take the 12 slices of whole grain bread and drizzle olive oil over them, then give about 2 shakes of the Italian seasoning. Place them on a baking sheet and place under a hot boiler until they are toasted to a light golden brown, a couple of minutes. Flip over and repeat the above. Remove from oven and set aside to cool. When cooled, cut into fine "bread crumbs." You can put into a food processor for a few seconds to make the fine breadcrumbs.

Preheat the oven to 350 degrees Fahrenheit. In a bowl beat the 2 eggs with a whisk. Dip each slice of eggplant in the eggs, then in the fine breadcrumbs. Pour the 6 cups of spaghetti sauce into a 9x13 inch baking pan. Place half of the crusted eggplant slices in the bottom; sprinkle 2 cups of shredded mozzarella cheese and 1/4 cup of grated Parmesan Cheese. Repeat the layers and then sprinkle the 1/2 teaspoon of dried basil over the top. Bake until a nice crusty golden brown, about 35 minutes.

Mexican Chicken

This delicious chicken meal satisfies those south of the border cravings. Makes 4 servings.

What You'll Need:

4 servings of cooked rice
4 chicken breast halves (boneless, skinless)
1 can of black beans (15 oz., drained, rinsed)
1 can of tomatoes with green chili peppers (diced, 10 oz.)
1 can of corn (whole kernels, 8.75 oz., drained)
1 tablespoon of canola oil
Pinch of cumin (ground)

How to Make It:

Add the tablespoon of canola oil to a large skillet and turn to medium high. Cook the 4 boneless, skinless chicken breast halves until lightly browned on all sides. Stir in the 1 can of black beans (15 oz., drained, rinsed), 1 can of tomatoes with green chili peppers (diced, 10 oz.), and the 1 can of corn (whole kernels, 8.75 oz., drained). Turn the heat to medium low and simmer for half an hour. Add the pinch of ground cumin prior to serving over a bed of rice.

Orange Lime Shrimp

This is a tangy shrimp recipe that is simple to make and delicious to eat. Serve with vegetables and rice.

What You'll Need:

1 1/2 pounds of shrimp (peeled, deveined, large)
2/3 cup of orange juice
1/3 cup of lime juice
2 tablespoons of orange zest
2 tablespoons of olive oil
1 tablespoon of lime zest
1 1/2 teaspoon of garlic (minced)
1/2 teaspoon of salt

How to Make It:

Add the 2/3 cup of orange juice, 1/3 cup of lime juice, 2 tablespoons of orange zest, 2 tablespoons of olive oil, 1 tablespoon of lime zest, 1 1/2 teaspoon of garlic (minced), and 1/2 teaspoon of salt to a blender or food processor and blend until smooth. Pour into a bowl and toss in the 1 1/2 pounds of peeled deveined shrimp and let sit for 20 minutes, on the countertop. Place a non-stick skillet on the stove and turn to medium high. Cook each shrimp for several minutes until it turns opaque.

Baste with the marinade while they cook. Serve immediately.

Orange Roughy

This is a different twist for orange roughy with a touch of lemon and orange. Makes 4 servings.

What You'll Need:

4 orange roughy fillets
2 tablespoons of orange juice
2 tablespoons of lemon juice
1 tablespoon of olive oil
1/2 teaspoon of lemon pepper

How to Make It:

Place the tablespoon of olive oil in a skillet and heat to medium high. Add the 4 orange roughy fillets and cook for a couple of minutes, then drizzle with the 2 tablespoons of orange juice and the 2 tablespoons of lemon juice. Sprinkle with the 1/2 teaspoon of lemon pepper. Cook until the fish is flaky.

Spicy Black Beans and Quinoa

This is a delicious dish filled with super foods, packed with nutrition and flavor.

What You'll Need:

2 cans of black beans (15 oz., drained, rinsed)
1 1/2 cups of vegetable stock
1 cup of corn (frozen)
3/4 cup of quinoa (uncooked)
1/2 cup of cilantro (fresh chopped)
1/2 cup of onion (chopped)
1 1/2 teaspoons of garlic (minced)
1 teaspoon of cumin (ground)
1 teaspoon of canola oil
1/4 teaspoon of cayenne pepper
Salt and pepper

How to Make It:

Pour the teaspoon of canola oil in mid-sized saucepan and heat to medium. Add the 1/2 cup of chopped onions and the 1 1/2 teaspoons of minced garlic and sauté. Stir in the 3/4 cup of uncooked quinoa and the 1 1/2 cups of vegetable stock. Sprinkle in the 1 teaspoon of cumin (ground), 1 teaspoon of canola oil, 1/4 teaspoon of cayenne pepper, and dashes of salt and pepper. Turn the heat to high and bring to a boil. Cover and reduce to low and simmer for about 20 minutes. Add the cup of frozen corn, stir, and cook for another 5 minutes. Add the 2 15 oz. cans of drained, rinsed black beans and the 1/2 cup of fresh chopped cilantro. Cook until heated through and serve.

Sweet and Tangy Tilapia

Fish lovers will enjoy this sweet and tangy tilapia. Makes 4 servings.

What You'll Need:

1 pound of tilapia (fillets)
1 butternut squash (sliced)
1 bunch of asparagus (fresh, trimmed)
1/2 cup of mozzarella cheese (shredded)
1/4 cup of honey
3 tablespoons of lime juice
1 teaspoon of garlic (minced)
Salt and pepper
Poultry seasoning

How to Make It:

Combine the 1/4 cup of honey, 3 tablespoons of lime juice, and 1 teaspoon of garlic (minced) in a bowl. Sprinkle salt and pepper on the tilapia and add to the marinade, turning the fish to coat. Refrigerate for an hour.
Preheat the oven to 350 degrees Fahrenheit. Spray a baking dish (large enough to lay the tilapia in) with cooking spray. Add the sliced butternut squash and the

fresh trimmed asparagus in the bottom of the baking dish. Place the marinated fish on top. Sprinkle with dashes of poultry seasoning. Bake in the hot oven until the fish is flaky and the vegetables are tender, about 20 minutes. Add the 1/2 cup of shredded mozzarella cheese on top and bake another 5 minutes, until the cheese melts. Serve immediately.

Tuna Salad

This is a refreshingly light main dish, makes a perfect lunch too. Makes 4 servings.

What You'll Need:

2 cans of tuna (6oz, packed in water, drained)
2 scallions (chopped)
1 apple (cored, cut into bite sizes)
8 cups of spinach (fresh chopped)
2/3 cup of cranberries (dried)
1/4 cup of mayonnaise
Salt and pepper

How to Make It:

Combine the 2 cans of tuna (6oz, packed in water, drained), 2 scallions (chopped), 1 apple (cored, cut into bite sizes), 2/3 cup of cranberries (dried), 1/4 cup of mayonnaise, and dashes of salt and pepper in a bowl. Divide the 8 cups of spinach (fresh chopped) in 4 plates. Divide the tuna salad over the fresh chopped spinach and serve.

1Turkey Chili

This is another version of a delicious comfort food made with chili. Makes 6 servings.

What You'll Need:

1.5 lbs. of ground turkey
1 bell pepper (green, chopped)
1 can of tomatoes (28 oz., diced)
1 can of black beans (19 oz., drained)
1 can of corn (15.25 oz., whole kernel, undrained)
Dashes of chili powder
Dashes of cinnamon (ground)
Dashes of cumin (ground)
Dashes of red pepper flakes

How to Make It:

Cook the 1.5 lbs. of ground turkey in a skillet on medium heat. Transfer the browned ground turkey to a large saucepan and add the 1 bell pepper (green, chopped), 1 can of tomatoes (28 oz., diced), 1 can of black beans (19 oz., drained), 1 can of corn (15.25 oz., whole kernel, undrained), dashes of chili powder , dashes of cinnamon (ground), dashes of cumin (ground), and dashes of red pepper flakes. Stir and turn the heat to high to bring to a boil. Reduce heat to simmer for half an hour.

Turkey Meatloaf

Turkey is a good lean meat and if you love meatloaf, you will love this recipe. Makes 5 servings.

What You'll Need:

1/2 pound of ground turkey
1 egg
1/2 cup of salsa (divided)
1/4 cup of onions (chopped)
1/4 cup of bread crumbs (from whole grain bread)
1/8 cup of bell pepper (chopped red)
1/8 cup of bell pepper (chopped yellow)

How to Make It:

Prep: Preheat the oven to 350 degrees Fahrenheit. Line a loaf pan with foil and lightly spray with cooking spray.

Add the 1/2 pound of ground turkey, 1 egg, 1/4 cup of salsa, 1/4 cup of onions (chopped), 1/4 cup of bread crumbs (from whole grain bread), 1/8 cup of bell pepper (chopped red), and 1/8 cup of bell pepper (chopped yellow) and mix with bare hands. Mold into a loaf and place in the loaf pan. Pour the remaining 1/4 cup of salsa over the top and bake until well done, when a meat thermometer reaches 165 degrees Fahrenheit, about 25 minutes.

Section 2: Intermittent Fasting Diet

What is the intermittent fasting diet?

This is a diet in which you eat during specified time frames. There are two popular versions of this diet. One being a day to day eat and fast where you eat on day one, fast on day two, and repeat until the desired weight is lost. The other version is a daily fasting, where you eat for a six to eight hour and then fast the rest of the day.

Starting out on the intermittent fasting diet

Please be aware that results from the intermittent diet vary from person to person. Much of the variance depends upon the build of the body, how much fat, and weight need to be lost and how they eat during the diet. Other factors that influence weight loss are lifestyle (do you smoke? drink? eat excessive junk food?), insulin resistance, exercise or not, and work. All these things work towards either making it difficult to lose the weight or to lose it fast. No two people are alike, even if they each desire to lose the same amount of weight. Keeping this in mind helps you to tailor the diet to your own needs.

Intermittent means eating and fasting in chunks of time. You may need to adjust this as you go along, to help deal with other health issues, to speed things along or to help improve health. Be ready to make adjustments and learn how to bend with the changes. Keeping a positive attitude will carry you a long ways in having good success in this diet.

This is a great diet to start for good weight loss. When the weight and fat are gone you can go on a maintenance, where you may still continue to fast, but more on a less restriction.

Other Issues Helped By Intermittent Fasting

If you suffer from any type of insulin or blood sugar problems, the metabolism is improved by fasting, eating in this manner. Eating through a fasting manner helps the body to lower inflammation rates, helps to improve blood pressure, helps to release stress, and helps to boost the immune system. If the immune system is boosted, the body is able to fight off other illnesses and keep you healthy and strong. Because this diet helps also to increase metabolism (especially if you eat the right food) you will have more energy to exercise and your body will have more energy to digest and disperse the foods you eat.

One of the biggest reasons people gain so much weight is they feel the need to eat all the time. This constant eating causes people to grab for the fast, convenient, and high in sugar and salt foods. These foods are responsible for putting a massive amount of weight on those who gorge. The intermittent fasting diet stops this binge eating and helps to creating a habit of eating during the best times of the day.

The Basics of the Intermittent Fasting Diet

The intermittent fasting diet is an extremely flexible diet plan. There are no set rules for doing it other than having a nice solid block of time to fast. As mentioned above one of the methods of fasting involves taking a day or longer of no food, and doing this a couple of times a week. For obvious reasons, this mode is a lot tougher to deal with, as going a solid day without food may be impossible for some people, especially for those with blood sugar issues.

Daily intermittent fasting is better because it does allow for the intake of food on a daily basis. But it also means for a strict window of daily fasting too and this is what helps to facilitate the weight loss. Basically you eat during a six to eight hour time and fast the remainder.

Your lifestyle will directly affect the effectiveness of this diet. Because the diet is flexible, there are no set foods or meals to eat during the six to eight hour window, just to eat. If you are in the habit of consuming a lot of carbohydrates, (sugars, white flours, and basically food with no nutritious value) then your weight loss may not happen or may be very slow. If your lifestyle is very sedentary, it will take longer to lose the weight.

Here is the thing, if you clean up your eating habits and eat foods packed with nutrition, it will give your body the energy to burn to move about more. You will want to exercise and move about more. Your digestive system will also work more efficiently, digesting in a time and manner that will get rid of the fat and calories.

Choosing the Daily Intermittent Fasting

This book is geared to offer recipes for the daily plan. It is easier to follow the daily fasting routine and can be developed into a habit, which will help it to be easier to do. You will break bad habits of needing to binge or gorge on food, because you know that after your six to eight hours, you simply will not eat. Your body will be able to adjust to this much easier, because you will have food in your body daily. If you eat the right foods, your body will have nutrients in which to work to help keep you healthier.

Snacking is the downfall of many who may eat well during the meals but find themselves reaching for foods void of nutrients. Unfortunately, these types of foods are highly addictive, the more we consume them the more our bodies want it. But it is also a habit that is fairly easy to break if you have the will power to do so. This diet stops the constant snacking.

By fasting on a daily basis, you will be more aware of your body. The hope is you will be aware of the foods you eat during the feeding hours, and will choose to consume healthier foods and snacks.

Be Aware Of Issues

If you do not consume enough calories during the feeding window, you can run the risk of reaching a weight loss plateau. This occurs when the body is too restricted from food (remember what we discussed about "starvation mode" above?) This can be avoided by eating the right foods. If you consume junk foods, then your body will not have substantial energy to keep going during the fasting period. If you eat a balance of good complex carbohydrates, proteins, and nutrients, your body can easily sustain the diet and the body during the fasting.

Some people will not be able to do the intermittent fasting diet. Some people have a greater need for more calories and they simply will not perform well unless they are consuming these calories. It is wise to have a physical and make sure your body can handle such a diet. Go over your choices with your health care provider and let them help you to decide whether or not this diet is right and healthy for you.

Making the Intermittent Diet a Success

This diet can be a great success if you do it right. It does take work and dedication though. First thing is to eat right. Choose foods that are healthy and whole during your feeding and avoid junk foods altogether. Eat a good breakfast each morning that will fuel your body to keep it going during the day. Choose healthy snacks. In the sample 5 day meal plan we suggest to eat fruit and nuts to snack. It is okay to drink fruit juice and eat leftovers or a small meal if you would rather. The point is to consume foods like lean meats, fruits, vegetables, and whole grains that help to give the body all the nutrients it needs to function at optimum levels.

Once the feeding window closes, do not consume any more food until the next day. It is okay and encouraged, though, to drink plenty of water throughout the entire day. Water helps to facilitate weight loss and helps to cleanse the body of impurities and toxins. Try drinking water throughout the feeding window as well. It helps with digestion too.

Take up an exercise routine. If your body is moving around it helps to burn more calories. Exercise also helps the body to release endorphins, and these are nature's way of giving you a natural high. Exercise is addictive too, the more you do it the more you will want to do it. The toughest part is starting. Even if you only work out three times a week for thirty minutes each time, you are giving your body a greater chance of fat and weight loss by doing so.

Sample 5 Day Meal Plan

The three meals here are smaller portions than a regular meal. The meals are to be eaten in a 6 to 8 hour time frame, with a 16 to 18 time frame of fasting. During the fasting time, you can have water. It is okay to have more with the meals if you are hungry. Try having a salad with lunch and supper if needed. Drink plenty of water during the day too.

Day One

Breakfast - Tomato Spinach Eggs
Snack - Nuts
Lunch - Edamame and Grilled Salmon
Snack - Fruit
Supper - Apple and Turkey Ham Salad

Day Two

Breakfast - Whole Grain Hot Cereal with Cherries
Snack - Nuts
Lunch - Balsamic Turkey Meatloaf
Snack - Fruit
Supper - Broccoli Cheese Soup

Day Three

Breakfast - Savory Hash Browns
Snack - Nuts
Lunch Buffalo Chicken with Slaw
Snack - Fruit
Supper - Open Face Tomato and Mozzarella Herb Sandwich

Day Four

Breakfast - Mexican Breakfast Casserole
Snack - Nuts
Lunch - Shrimp Scampi
Snack - Fruit
Supper - Spinach Salad with Pomegranate Dressing

Day Five

Breakfast - Healthy Breakfast Burrito
Snack - Nuts
Lunch - Italian Chicken
Snack - Fruit
Supper - Baked Potatoes Twice

Intermittent Fasting Diet Recipes

Intermittent Fasting Diet Breakfast Recipes

Breakfast Casserole

This makes a perfect brunch because it is a hearty and filling casserole of eggs, cheese, tomatoes, and English muffins. This recipe needs to be prepared the night before. Makes 8 servings.

What You'll Need:

4 English muffins (halved, toasted)
4 scallions (cut into long bite-sized pieces)
4 eggs plus 3 egg whites
3 cups of milk (low fat)
2/3 cup of cheddar cheese (extra sharp, shredded, divided)
3/4 cup of deli ham (torn, thin slices)
1/2 cup of tomatoes (no oil, sundried, sliced)
1 tablespoon of Dijon mustard

Salt and pepper

How to Make It:

Spray a 2-quart baking dish with cooking spray. Layer the bottom of the pan with the 4 halved and toasted English muffins and the 3/4 cup of torn thin sliced deli ham, making sure to lay it out evenly.   Next layer it with the 4 scallions cut into bite-sized pieces, 1/2 cup of sliced sundried tomatoes, and 1/3 cup of shredded extra sharp cheddar cheese. In a bowl, crack the 4 eggs and add the 3 egg whites and beat with a whisk, then combine with the 3 cups of low fat milk, tablespoon of Dijon mustard and dashes of salt and pepper. Pour the egg mixture over the layered casserole in the baking dish. Add the remaining 1/3 cup of extra sharp cheddar cheese on top. Cover tightly with plastic wrap and refrigerate overnight. Next morning, preheat the oven to 350 degrees Fahrenheit. Remove the plastic wrap and cook the casserole (with a baking sheet under it) for 60 minutes. Remove from oven and let it sit for at least 10 minutes to set and cool before serving and enjoying.

Healthy Breakfast Burrito

Mornings are the time to refuel for the day. Start the day right with a breakfast burrito that is as healthy as it is delicious. Makes 4 servings.

What You'll Need:

4 tortillas (whole wheat, burrito)
4 eggs
4 egg whites
1 avocado (cubed)
1 cup of onions (diced)
1 cup of black beans (cooked, rinsed)
3/4 cup of tomatoes (diced)
1/2 cup of bell peppers (red, seeded, diced)
1/3 cup of pepper Jack cheese (shredded)
1/4 cup of sour cream
1/4 cup of salsa
2 teaspoons of canola oil
1/4 teaspoon of red pepper flakes
Salt and pepper
Hot sauce

How to Make It:

Add the 2 teaspoons of canola oil to a skillet on medium

high heat. Sauté the 1/2 cup of seeded, diced red bell peppers and 1/2 cup of diced onions. Stir in the cup of cooked, rinsed black beans and the 1/4 teaspoon of red pepper flakes. Cook for a couple of minutes to warm, and then add dashes of salt and pepper. Put the contents into a bowl and set aside. In a separate bowl crack the 4 eggs and add the additional 4 egg whites and whisk. Add the 1/3 cup of shredded pepper Jack cheese. Spray the same skillet with cooking spray, heat to medium and scramble the eggs until done. In a separate non-stick skillet, heat to medium, and warm each tortilla on each side for about 30 seconds. Next, to build the burrito, add 1/4 of the sour cream and 1/4 of the salsa followed by 1/4 of the black beans and topped with 1/4 of the eggs and then season with extra salt, pepper, and hot sauce. Roll up and serve. Do this with each one.

Mexican Style Eggs "Huevos Rancheros"

If you love Mexican food, you will love your breakfast fixed fiesta style. Makes 4 servings.

What You'll Need:

4 eggs
4 tortillas (corn, 6 inch, warmed)
1 can of black beans (15.5 oz, drained, rinsed)
1 jalapeno pepper (minced)
1 1/2 cups of tomatoes (fine chopped)
1/2 cup of onions (fine chopped)
1/2 cup of feta cheese (crumbled)
1/2 cup of water (warm)
1/4 cup of cilantro (fresh chopped)
2 tablespoons of olive oil (plus 2 teaspoons, extra virgin)
1 teaspoon of garlic (minced)
1 teaspoon of cumin (ground)
1/2 teaspoon of hot sauce
Salt and pepper

How to Make It:

Mix the 1 jalapeno pepper (minced), 1 1/2 cups of tomatoes (fine chopped), 1/2 cup of onions (fine chopped), 1 teaspoon of garlic (minced), 1 teaspoon of cumin (ground), 1/2 teaspoon of hot sauce, and dashes of salt and pepper together to make salsa. Pour 2 teaspoons of olive oil into a skillet and heat to medium low. Pour in the "salsa" mixture and stir for a couple of minutes until it thickens. Pour the salsa in a bowl and set to the side. Add the can of drained, rinsed black beans along with 1/2 cup of warm water and another dash of salt into the skillet. Cover, turn heat to low and simmer while preparing the rest of the eggs. Add the 2 tablespoons of extra virgin olive oil to another skillet and heat to medium. Crack the eggs, one at a time to make 4 fried eggs, or sunny side up. Season with salt and pepper. Warm the 4 tortillas by placing on a plate with a damp paper towel on top and microwave for about 20 seconds. Next, place a tortilla on 4 plates. Equally divide the beans on top of the 4 tortillas. Add a fried egg to each one. Add a spoon of salsa on top of each egg, and then divide the 1/2 cup of feta cheese crumbles on top of the salsa. Garnish with the 1/4 cup of fresh chopped cilantro and the rest of the salsa. Serve immediately.

Mexican Breakfast Casserole

Here is a casserole filled with the spiciness of chili and cilantro, delicious and filling. Makes 6 servings.

What You'll Need:

4 cups of tortilla chips (baked, divided)
4 eggs plus 6 extra egg whites
1 can of green chilies (chopped, drained)
1/2 cup of cheddar cheese (sharp, shredded - divided)
1/2 cup of pepper Jack cheese (shredded - divided)
1/2 cup of salsa (green Verde)
1/4 cup of skim milk
1 tablespoon of cilantro (fresh chopped plus more for garnishment)
3/4 teaspoon of ancho chili powder
Dollops of sour cream
Salt and pepper

How to Make It:

Prep: Preheat the oven to 375 degrees Fahrenheit. Spray a 2 quart baking dish with cooking spray.

Crumble the 4 cups of baked tortilla chips (large crumbles) and lay 2 cups of chips in the bottom of the baking dish. In a bowl, crack the 4 eggs and add the 6 egg whites and beat with a whisk. Add the 1/4 cup of skim milk, 3/4 teaspoon of ancho chili powder, and dashes of salt and pepper and stir. Mix in the can of chopped drained green chilies, 1/4 cup of shredded sharp cheddar cheese, 1/4 cup of shredded pepper Jack cheese, and the tablespoon of fresh chopped cilantro. Pour the mixture over the baked tortilla chips in the baking dish. Place in hot oven and bake for about 22 minutes, until the eggs are set. Pull out of oven and sprinkle the remaining 1/4 cup of shredded sharp cheddar cheese and the 1/4 cup of shredded pepper Jack cheese and place back in the oven for 10 more minutes. Pull from oven, turn heat off, and allow sitting for another 10 minutes. Serve with a spoon of green Verde salsa, dollop of sour cream, and a garnishment of cilantro leaf.

Savory Hash Browns

All you need to do is cook up and egg and have a piece of whole grain toast and you are set for a meal. Makes 4 servings.

What You'll Need:

2 potatoes (Yukon gold, washed, grated - with skins)
2 scallions (chopped)
1 parsnip (peeled, grated)
2 tablespoons of parsley (minced flat leaf)
1 tablespoon of olive oil (extra virgin, divided)
Salt and pepper

How to Make It:

Toss the 2 grated potatoes with the grated parsnip, add the 2 chopped scallions, greens and all. Season with dashes of salt and pepper. Pour the 1/2 tablespoon of extra virgin olive oil into a skillet and heat to medium. Stir in the grated potatoes, parsnips, and scallions, tossing to coat with oil, then press down into the skillet, once in a while, run the spatula under the mixture to prevent sticking. Cook until crispy brown for around 10 minutes. Flip the mixture out onto a large dinner plate. Add the remaining 1/2 tablespoon of olive oil, return skillet to heat, then replace the mixture, uncooked side down to crisp the other side, another 10 minutes. Serve hot.

Squash, Zucchini and Eggs

This is a great summer meal using fresh squash if possible. Makes 6 servings.

What You'll Need:

6 eggs
4 scallions (sliced thin, greens separated out)
3 squash (grated)
3 zucchini (grated)
1 jalapeno (seeded, minced)
1/4 cup of cheddar cheese (sharp white, shredded)
1/4 cup of pepper jack (shredded)
3 tablespoons of parsley (fresh chopped)
2 tablespoons of olive oil (extra virgin)
1 tablespoon of butter
1 tablespoon of salt
1/4 teaspoon of nutmeg (ground)
Salt and pepper

How to Make It:

Toss the 3 shredded squash and the 3 grated zucchinis with a tablespoon of salt while they rest in a colander for 35 minutes. Using a paper towel, squeeze the squash and zucchini.

Preheat the oven to 375 degrees Fahrenheit. Place an oven proof (cast iron works well) skillet on the stove on medium high heat. Pour in the 2 tablespoons of extra virgin olive oil. Reserve 3 tablespoons of the greens from the 4 scallions and put the remainder of the greens and all the whites into the heated oil along with the seeded minced jalapeno and sauté. Toss in the grated squash and zucchini, stir, and toss for about 7 minutes. Add the 3 tablespoons of fresh chopped parsley, 1/4 teaspoon of ground nutmeg, and dashes of salt, pepper, and stir, cooking for another minute. Remove skillet from the stove and sit for 5 minutes away from the heat. Next, pat the squash, zucchini mixture down, then with the back of a serving spoon make 6 indentions, spaced evenly over the squash and zucchini. Place 1/2 of a teaspoon of butter into each of the 6 indentions. Carefully, crack an egg in a cup, then pour right into and indention, with all 6 eggs. Sprinkle dashes of salt and pepper over the eggs. Add the remaining 1/4 cups of shredded sharp cheddar cheese and pepper Jack cheese, evenly over the top. Carefully place the skillet in the hot oven and bake for about 11 minutes. Garnish with the 3 tablespoons of the chopped green scallions and serve immediately.

Tomato Spinach Eggs

This is a delicious way to get protein and vegetables first thing in the morning, with this savory eggs Benedict recipe. Makes 4 servings.

What You'll Need:

8 cups of spinach (fresh baby)
4 slices of tomato (large slices)
4 eggs
2 English Muffins (split in half)
1/2 cup of onions (thin sliced)
1/3 cup of Canadian bacon (chunked)
1/4 cup of vinegar (white distilled)
2 tablespoons of mayonnaise
1 tablespoon of water (warm)
1 tablespoon of olive oil
2 teaspoons of mustard
1 teaspoon of lemon juice
Dash of cayenne pepper
Pepper

How to Make It:

Make the sauce by combining the 2 tablespoons of mayonnaise, 1 tablespoon of water (warm), 2 teaspoons of mustard, 1 teaspoon of lemon juice, and dash of cayenne pepper with a whisk.

Next, start the Benedict eggs by adding several inches of water to a large saucepan. Pour in the 1/4 cup of white distilled vinegar and turn the heat to medium.

Set a nonstick frying pan on medium high, add the tablespoon of olive oil, 1/3 cup of Canadian bacon chunks, and the 1/2 cup of onions, and cook until heated through. Stir in the 8 cups of fresh baby spinach, take the frying pan off the heat, and continue stirring for a couple of minutes until the leaves wilt. Sprinkle pepper and toss.

Pop the English muffins into a toaster to toast lightly on all sides. Set them on a serving platter and top with a slice of tomato. Add 1/4 of the Canadian bacon mixture on top of each tomato slice.

Next, cook one egg at a time, buy cracking into a small dish, then pouring into the simmering vinegar water. Cook for about 4 minutes. Remove and place on top of the Canadian bacon on the English muffin halves. Do this with all 4 eggs. Spoon the hollandaise sauce over the top and serve hot.

Whole Grain Hot Cereal with Cherries

There is nothing heartier than a bowl of hot whole grain cereal first thing in the morning. You will enjoy this meal with the aroma and flavor of fruit making it a delightful meal. Makes 4 servings.

What You'll Need:

5 cups of water
1/2 cup of rice (wild)
1/2 cup of oats (steel-cut)
1/2 cup of wheat cereal (cream of wheat)
1/4 cup of pearl barley
1/4 cup of cherries (dried)
1 cinnamon stick
1 1/2 tablespoons of brown sugar (packed)
1/2 teaspoon of orange zest
1/4 teaspoon of salt
Walnuts (chopped)
Butter
Milk

How to Make It:

The evening before add the 5 cups of water, 1/2 cup of rice (wild), 1/2 cup of oats (steel-cut), 1/2 cup of wheat cereal (cream of wheat), 1/4 cup of pearl barley, 1/4 cup of cherries (dried), 1 cinnamon stick, 1 1/2 tablespoons of brown sugar (packed), 1/2 teaspoon of orange zest, and 1/4 teaspoon of salt and stir in a large sauce pan. Place the cover and let sit on the stove with the heat off over night. The morning of breakfast, turn the stove on high and bring to a boil, then turn it down on low to simmer, cover on for 20 minutes. Keep the cover on, turn the stove off and let it sit for another 5 minutes. Serve in bowls and garnish with chopped walnuts, butter and milk if desired.

Whole Wheat Pancakes with Apples

Pancakes are always fun to cook and eat. You cannot go wrong with this recipe, which uses whole-wheat flour to give you the benefit of whole grains, and the goodness of fresh apples. Makes 6 servings.

What You'll Need:

1 cup of buttermilk (low fat)
3/4 cup of skim milk
3/4 cup of apples (cored, diced)
3/4 cup of flour (all-purpose)
3/4 cup of flour (whole-wheat)
2 eggs
6 tablespoons of maple syrup
1 tablespoon of honey
2 teaspoons of baking powder
1/2 teaspoon of baking soda
1/4 teaspoon of salt

How to Make It:

Prep: Preheat the oven to 250 degrees Fahrenheit.

In a bowl, combine the 3/4 cup of flour (all-purpose), 3/4 cup of flour (whole-wheat), 2 teaspoons of baking powder, 1/2 teaspoon of baking soda, and 1/4 teaspoon of salt. Crack the 2 eggs and beat with a whisk in a cup. In a separate bowl, combine the 1-cup of buttermilk (low fat), 3/4 cup of skim milk, beaten eggs, and the tablespoon of honey. Gradually add the dry ingredients, do not over stir.

Next, place the diced apples in a microwave safe dish, cover with plastic wrap, and microwave on normal for 2 minutes to soften.

Turn the heat to medium on a non-stick skillet or griddle. Ladle out about a fourth a cup of batter onto the hot surface. Spoon a couple of apples over the top, flip after a couple of minutes. Repeat until all the batter and apples are gone. Drizzle with the maple syrup or your favorite syrup over the top, or sprinkle cinnamon and sugar over the top.

Zucchini Frittata

This delicious breakfast would make a good dinner choice too, as it's healthy and filling, full of feta cheese, zucchini, potatoes and turkey bacon. Makes 4 servings.

What You'll Need:

4 eggs + 2 egg whites
2 strips of turkey bacon (cooked, crumbled)
1 zucchini (grated and dried with a towel)
1 cup of potatoes (russet, cubed)
1/2 cup of feta cheese
1/2 cup of onion (chopped fine)
2 tablespoons of cilantro (fresh chopped)
1 tablespoon of olive oil
3/4 teaspoon of salt
1/2 teaspoon of garlic (minced)
1/4 teaspoon of hot sauce

How to Make It:

Add the 1 cup of cubed potatoes to a saucepan and cover with water, bring to a boil on high heat, then turn down to medium high. Cook for about 7 minutes or until the potatoes are tender enough to eat. Remove from heat, drain the water and place in a bowl. Using a paper towel, dry the potato cubes.

In a bowl, add the 4 eggs and 2 egg whites and beat with a whisk. Stir in the cup of cilantro, 3/4 teaspoon of salt, and 1/4 teaspoon of hot sauce.

Turn the on the oven broiler to high.

Place an ovenproof skillet on the stove (about a 10 inch size) and turn to medium high heat. Add the tablespoon of olive oil and sauté the 1/2 cup of fine chopped onion and the 1/2 teaspoon of minced garlic. Stir in the grated zucchini and cook for another 5 minutes. Stir in the cooked potato cubes, browning them for about 4 minutes. Next, pour the whisked egg mixture over the potatoes and zucchini. Place the skillet back on medium heat, lifting the edges to allow the egg to run, for a couple of minutes. Next, sprinkle the 2 strips of crumbled turkey bacon and the 1/2 cup of feta cheese over the top and place under the broiler for 5 minutes. Serve hot.

Intermittent Fasting Diet Dinner Recipes

Balsamic Turkey Meatloaf

If you are a meatloaf lover you will enjoy this different twist for meatloaf, which is a bit healthier than the beef counterpart. Makes 8 servings.

What You'll Need:

1.5 pounds of ground turkey
1 zucchini (fine diced)
1 bell pepper (red fine diced)
1 bell pepper (yellow fine diced)
1 egg
1 cup of bread crumbs
3/4 cup of ketchup (divided)
1/4 cup + 2 tablespoons of balsamic vinegar
1/4 cup of Parmesan cheese (grated)
1/4 cup of Romano cheese (grated)
1/4 cup of parsley (fresh chopped)
2 tablespoons of olive oil (extra-virgin)
1 tablespoon of thyme (fresh fine chopped)
2 1/2 teaspoons of garlic (minced)
1/2 teaspoon of red pepper flakes
Salt and pepper

How to Make It:

Prep: Preheat oven to 425 degrees Fahrenheit. Line a 9x5 inch loaf pan with foil.

Add the 2 tablespoons of extra virgin olive oil to a skillet on high heat and sauté the fine diced zucchini, red and yellow bell peppers, 2 1/2 teaspoons of minced garlic and dashes of salt and pepper for about 5 minutes. Set aside.

Crack the egg in a bowl and beat with a whisk, and stir in the 1/4 cup of fresh chopped parsley and the tablespoon of fresh fine chopped thyme. Add the 1.5 pounds of ground turkey, breaking it up with your hands, along with the cup of breadcrumbs, 1/4 cup of grated Parmesan cheese, 1/4 cup of grated Romano cheese, 1/2 cup of ketchup, 2 tablespoons of balsamic vinegar, and the zucchini and bell peppers. Mix with bare hands and mold into a loaf. Add to the lined loaf pan. Make the sauce for the topping by mixing the 1/4 cup of ketchup with the 1/4 cup of balsamic vinegar and the 1/2 teaspoon of red pepper flakes, and dashes of salt and pepper. Stir with a whisk, and then pour over the top of the meat loaf. Cook for 1 hour and 15 minutes, until the internal temperature of the meatloaf reaches 165 degrees Fahrenheit with a meat thermometer.

Buffalo Chicken with Slaw

Buffalo chicken is always associated as an appetizer but here it is a delicious main meal with a side of fresh homemade slaw. Makes 4 servings.

What You'll Need:

4 chicken breast halves (boneless, skinless, cut into strips)
4 cups of cabbage (shredded)
2 cups of buttermilk
2 cups of carrots (grated)
2 cups of bread crumbs (fine)
1 cup of celery (thin sliced)
1/2 cup of canola oil
1/2 cup of mayonnaise
1/2 cup of sour cream
1/2 cup of blue cheese (crumbles)
2 tablespoons of hot sauce (divided)
Salt and pepper

How to Make It:

Combine the 2 cups of buttermilk with 1 tablespoon of hot sauce and dashes of salt and pepper. Put the 4 boneless, skinless chicken breast halves cut into strips into a shallow dish. Pour the buttermilk mixture over the chicken, cover and refrigerate for 60 minutes. Combine the 1/2 cup of mayonnaise with the 1/2 cup of sour cream and the 1/2 cup of blue cheese crumbles in a blender or food processor until nice and lump free (this is the dressing). Using a whisk, add the remaining tablespoon of hot sauce and mix. In a bowl, add the 4 cups of shredded cabbage, 2 cups of grated carrots, with the 1 cup of thin sliced celery and toss. Pour 3/4 cup of the dressing over the cabbage mixture and toss to coat all. There will be 1/4 cup of dressing left over for a dipping sauce.

Add the 2 cups of fine bread crumbs to a shallow dish. Shake each chicken strip from the marinade and roll in the bread crumbs. Pour the 1/2 cup of canola oil into a skillet and turn to medium high heat. Fry each coated chicken strip for 4 minutes, turn and cook another 4 minutes, until all the chicken is cooked.

Serve with a side of slaw and dip in the dressing.

Edamame and Grilled Salmon

It is hard to beat salmon in terms of nutrition and flavor. This delicious meal is savory to the palate the filling. Makes 4 servings.

What You'll Need:

4 salmon fillets (skin on)
2 scallions (fine chopped)
1 1/3 cup of Edamame (cooked)
1/4 cup of cilantro leaves (fresh fine chopped)
2 teaspoons of canola oil
2 teaspoons of lime juice
2 teaspoons of soy sauce
2 teaspoons of honey
1 teaspoon of ginger (grated)
1/4 teaspoon of sesame seeds (black)
Salt and pepper
lime wedges (for garnish)

How to Make It:

Prep: Preheat the grill to medium high. Rub canola oil on the grates.

Mix the 2 fine chopped scallions with the 1/4 cup of

fresh fine chopped cilantro leaves, 2 teaspoons of canola oil, and the teaspoon of grated ginger. Dash salt and pepper and toss. Cut into the middle of the skins of the salmon fillets, making 2 slits about three inches in length from top to bottom, cutting halfway into the salmon. Do so with each fillet, and evenly spoon the scallions and cilantro into each slit. Salt and pepper the rest of the salmon fillets. In a cup, mix the 2 teaspoons of lime juice, 2 teaspoons of soy sauce, with the 2 teaspoons of honey with a whisk. Gently set each salmon fillet on the grill with the skin / herbs side facing up. Grill for about 3 1/2 minutes. Flip the salmon, brush the top with the lime juice sauce mixture and grill for another 3 1/2 minutes. Place cooked salmon fillets on a serving platter; evenly sprinkle the 1/4 teaspoon of black sesame seeds over the tops. Garnish with the lime wedges and serve with the 1 1/3 cup of cooked Edamame in a serving dish.

Grilled Chicken Tostadas

This is a healthy meal made with tasty seasoned chicken breasts and a variety of other savory flavors. Makes 4 servings.

What You'll Need:

4 tortillas (flour, 8 inch)
2 chicken breasts (boneless, skinless, cut into bite-sized pieces)
1 pound of tomatillos (husked and rinsed)
4 lime wedges
1 chipotle chili in adobo sauce (chopped coarse)
2 cups of romaine lettuce (shredded)
1/3 cup of feta cheese (crumbled)
1/4 cup of lime juice
4 tablespoons of onions (fine chopped)
2 tablespoons of cilantro (fresh chopped)
1 tablespoon of olive oil
1 teaspoon of garlic (minced)
Salt

How to Make It:

In a large bowl, combine the 1/4 cup of lime juice with the coarse chopped chipotle chili in adobo sauce and dashes of salt. Toss in the 2 cut up boneless, skinless chicken breasts and cover. Refrigerate for 2 hours to marinate. Place the chicken pieces on greased skewers. Turn the grill to medium heat. Spray the 4 8-inch flour tortillas with cooking spray and grill them for about 45 seconds, flip and grill another 45 seconds. Place the skewered chicken and the pound of husked, rinsed tomatillos on the grill and turn every 30 seconds for about 5 minutes. Remove the chicken and tomatillos from the heat. Remove the skewers from the chicken. Chop the grilled tomatillos into bite sized chunks in a bowl. Add the tablespoon of olive oil and a dash of salt and toss. Layer the tostadas by placing a tortilla down first, then divide the 2 cups of shredded romaine lettuce, tomatillos, chicken, 4 tablespoons of onions (fine chopped), and the 2 tablespoons of cilantro (fresh chopped). Garnish each plate with a lime wedge. Enjoy.

Italian Chicken

This savory Italian Chicken dish goes well with a salad or steamed vegetables. Makes 6 servings.

What You'll Need:

4 chicken breast halves (bone- in, skinless)
2 chicken thighs (skinless, bone-in)
1 can of tomatoes (diced, 15 oz)
3 oz of prosciutto (chopped)
1/2 cup of white grape juice
1/2 cup of chicken stock
1/2 cup of bell pepper (red, sliced)
1/2 cup of bell pepper (yellow, sliced)
1/4 cup of olive oil
1/4 cup of parsley (fresh flat leaf, chopped)
2 tablespoons of capers
1 tablespoon of thyme (fresh)
1 1/2 teaspoon of salt (divided)
1 teaspoon of oregano (fresh)
1 teaspoon of garlic (minced)
1/2 teaspoon of pepper

How to Make It:

Rinse and pat dry the chicken. Rub 1/2 teaspoons each

of salt and pepper on all of the chicken. Pour the 1/4 cup of olive oil in a skillet and turn to medium heat. Add the chicken to the hot oil and brown on each side. Place on a platter and set to the side. In the same skillet add the 1/2 cups of chopped yellow and red bell peppers and the 3 oz of chopped prosciutto and sauté. Stir in the teaspoon of minced garlic and cook for another 60 seconds. Add the 15 oz can of diced tomatoes, 1/2 cup of white grape juice, 1 tablespoon of thyme (fresh), 1 1/2 teaspoon of salt (divided), 1 teaspoon of oregano (fresh), and 1 teaspoon of garlic (minced). Deglaze the skillet by scraping the bits from the bottom into the mixture. Add the cooked chicken and pout in the 1/2 cup of chicken stock. Turn the heat to high and bring to a boil. Cover, reduce the heat to low and simmer for about 25 minutes. When cooked, stir in the 1/4 cup of fresh chopped flat leaf parsley and the 2 tablespoons of capers, then serve.

Oriental Turkey Burgers

Here is a different twist to an American favorite, turkey burgers seasoned up with oriental spices. Makes 4 burgers.

What You'll Need:

12 oz of ground turkey
4 hamburger buns (whole grain)
2 scallions (chopped)
1/2 cup of water (boiling)
1/2 cup of English cucumber (sliced thin)
1/4 cup of balsamic vinegar
1/4 cup of bulgur wheat
1/4 cup of yogurt (plain)
1/4 cup of cilantro (fresh whole)
1/8 cup of onion (sliced thin)
2 tablespoons of hoisin sauce
2 tablespoons of cilantro (fresh chopped)
2 teaspoons of canola oil
1 teaspoon of sugar (granulated)
1 teaspoon of ginger (grated)
1 teaspoon of chili garlic sauce
1/2 teaspoon of garlic (minced)
Salt and pepper

How to Make It:

First, combine the 1/2 cup of boiling water with the 1/4 cup of bulgur wheat in a small bowl. Seal with plastic wrap and set aside for about 50 minutes. Next, using a whisk in a separate bowl mix the 1/4 cup of balsamic vinegar with the teaspoon of granulated sugar. Toss in the 1/2 cup of thin sliced English cucumber and the 1/8 cup of thin sliced onions. Sprinkle with dashes of salt and pepper. Cover and set in refrigerator for half an hour. In another bowl, whisk together the 1/4 cup of plain yogurt with the teaspoon of chili garlic sauce and more dashes of salt and pepper.   Set the bowl aside while preparing the turkey. When the bulgur wheat is ready, drain the water and add the 12 oz of ground turkey, 2 chopped scallions, 2 tablespoons of hoisin sauce, 2 tablespoons of fresh chopped cilantro, teaspoon of grated ginger, and the 1/2 teaspoon of minced garlic. Mix with bare hands to insure good mixture. Separate into 4 patties. Add the 2 teaspoons of canola oil to a skillet and heat to medium high. Cook the turkey burgers until well done, 4 minutes on each side. Next, pour the cucumber mixture into a colander to drain, and then toss in the 1/4 cup of fresh whole cilantro leaves. Create the burgers by spreading the yogurt sauce onto each bun half, add the turkey burger, and then add a spoon of the cucumber cilantro mixture.

Enjoy.

Shepherd's Pie

This is a delicious and hearty one-dish meal. Makes 8 servings.

What You'll Need:

2 lbs. of potatoes (russet, scrubbed, peeled, chunked)
1.5 lbs. of ground beef (lean)
2 zucchinis (julienned)
8 oz. of mushrooms (button, sliced)
1 cup of carrots (peeled, grated)
1 cup of purple grape juice
1/2 cup of heavy cream
1/2 cup of bell pepper (red, julienned)
1/2 cup of Monterey Jack cheese (grated)
2 1/2 cup of beef stock (divided)
1/3 cup of butter
3/4 cup of onion (fine chopped, divided)
5 tablespoons of canola oil (divided)
3 tablespoons of flour (all-purpose)
2 tablespoons of tomato paste
2 teaspoons of Worcestershire sauce
1 teaspoon of paprika
1/2 teaspoon of cayenne pepper
1/2 teaspoon of garlic (minced)
Salt and pepper

Water

How to Make It:

Prep: Preheat the oven to 375 degrees Fahrenheit.

Add the 2 lbs. of scrubbed, peeled, chunked russet potatoes and the 1/2 teaspoon of minced garlic to a medium size saucepan and cover with water about an inch over the top of the potatoes. Dash some salt in the water and stir, turn heat to high and bring to a boil. Turn to medium high for about 15 minutes or until the potatoes are tender. Pour into a strainer to drain the water and return the potatoes to the saucepan. Add the 1/2 cup of heavy cream and the 3 tablespoons of butter and mash. Stir in dashes of salt and pepper and put aside.

In a large skillet add another tablespoon of butter with a tablespoon of canola oil and turn to medium high. Fry the 1.5 pounds of lean ground beef in the grease and add the 2 teaspoons of Worcestershire sauce and the 1/2 teaspoon of cayenne pepper and stir until the beef is well done. Season with dashes of salt and pepper. Add the 2 tablespoons of tomato sauce and stir over the heat. Pour in the 1/2 cup of beef stock and simmer for a few minutes. Pour the beef mixture in a large bowl and set aside. Add the remaining butter to the skillet and add 1/4 cup of fine chopped onions and sauté. Next add the 2 zucchinis (julienned), 1 cup of carrots (peeled, grated), 1/2 cup of bell pepper (red, julienned) and the teaspoon of paprika and stir. Cook an additional 10 minutes. Take off heat.

Create the pie by layering with 1/2 of the beef into the bottom of a 9x12 inch baking dish. Sprinkle the 1/2 cup of grated Monterey Jack cheese over the beef layer; add the remainder of the beef, pressing down firmly with a spoon back. Next, layer with the sautéed vegetables, and then add the mashed potatoes on top. Season the top with paprika and place in the oven to bake until the edges turn a golden brown, about 30 minutes.

While the pie is baking, make the gravy by pouring 3 tablespoons of canola oil into a saucepan and sautéing 1/4 cup of chopped onions and the 8 oz of sliced button mushrooms, until they are soft. Stir in the 3 tablespoons of all-purpose flour and using a whisk pour in the 2 cups of beef stock and the cup of purple grape juice and stir until it thickens. Season with salt and pepper as desired. Pour over slices of shepherd's pie and enjoy.

Shrimp Scampi

If you love shrimp, you will love this recipe, complete with whole grain noodles. Makes 4 servings.

What You'll Need:

16 shrimp (large, deveined, shelled)
6 oz of spaghetti noodles (whole grain)
6 black olives (pitted, chopped)
1/2 cup of onions (sliced thin)
1/4 cup of croutons (multi-grain, crumbed)
1/4 cup of parsley (fresh flat leaf, divided)
1/4 cup of chicken stock
1/4 cup of white grape juice
1 1/2 tablespoons of lemon zest (divided)
1 tablespoon of lemon juice
1 tablespoon of olive oil
1/2 teaspoon of garlic (minced)
1/4 teaspoon of red pepper flakes (crushed)
1/4 teaspoon of salt

How to Make It:

Cook the spaghetti noodles according to the directions on the package to "al dente." In a separate bowl, add the 1/4 cup of croutons (multi-grain, crumbed),

1/2 tablespoon of parsley (fresh flat leaf), and a tablespoon of the lemon zest and stir, let sit. Meanwhile, in a skillet, add the tablespoon of olive oil and turn to medium heat. Stir in the 1/2 cup of thin sliced onions, 1/2 teaspoon of garlic (minced), 1/4 teaspoon of red pepper flakes (crushed) and sauté for a minute. Stir in the 16 large deveined and shelled shrimp and the 1/4 teaspoon of salt and cook for another 90 seconds. Add the 1/4 cup of chicken stock, 1/4 cup of white grape juice, tablespoon of lemon juice and the 6 chopped, pitted black olives. Turn heat to high and bring to a boil, stirring and cooking for a minutes, then turn the heat back down to medium. Add the cook spaghetti noodles and the remainder of the parsley and lemon zest. Toss and pour into a serving dish. Sprinkle the 1/4 cup of crumbles multi-grain croutons over the top and serve.

Vegetable Pot Pie

Sometimes you simply do not need meat to make a full meal. This is a perfect tasty pot pie and all the better because it's homemade. Makes 8 servings.

What You'll Need:

2 pie crusts (9-inch deep dish, unbaked, rolled)
1 3/4 cup of vegetable stock
1 cup of carrots (thin sliced)
1 cup of English peas (frozen)
1 cup of potatoes (diced)
2/3 cup of milk
1/2 cup of celery (thin sliced)
1/2 cup of butter
1/3 cup of onion (fine chopped)
1/3 cup of flour (all-purpose, unbleached)
Salt and pepper
1/4 teaspoon of celery seed
1/4 teaspoon of garlic powder
Water

How to Make It:

Prep: Preheat the oven to 425 degrees Fahrenheit.

Place a saucepan over high heat and add 1 cup of carrots (thin sliced), 1 cup of English peas (frozen), 1 cup of potatoes (diced), and 1/2 cup of celery (thin sliced) and add enough water to cover the vegetables and bring the water to a boil. Add a lid and cook for 15 minutes, vegetables are done when they are tender. Drain water and set aside for a few minutes. Place a skillet on medium heat and add the 1/2 cup of butter and sauté the 1/3 cup of fine chopped onions. Add the 1/3 cup of flour (all-purpose, unbleached), dashes of salt and pepper, 1/4 teaspoon of celery seed, and 1/4 teaspoon of garlic powder and stir. Cook until well blended for a couple of minutes. Combine with the 1 3/4 cup of vegetable stock and the 2/3 cup of milk. Turn the heat to medium low and simmer for 5 more minutes. Turn off heat and stir in the cooked vegetables. Unroll a pie crust and place in a 9 inch deep dish pie pan. Add the vegetable mixture into the pie crust. Unroll the other pie crust and carefully place on top of the vegetable pie, sealing the edges but pressing a fork to make small ridges. Cut a couple of slits in the crust to vent the steam while cooking. Place on a baking sheet and in the oven for 35 minutes. Allow to sit to cool for about 10 minutes before serving.

Intermittent Fasting Diet Light Snack Recipes

Apple and Turkey Ham Salad

This is a delightfully crunchy sweet and savory salad. Makes 6 servings.

What You'll Need:

1/2 pound of turkey ham (thin sliced, torn)
4 endives (crosswise sliced)
3 apples (crisp, cored, sliced thin)
2 bunches of trimmed watercress
2 cups of onions (sliced thin)
1/4 cup of sour cream
1/4 cup of water
3 tablespoons of olive oil (extra virgin)
2 tablespoons of lemon juice
2 tablespoons of apple cider vinegar
2 tablespoons of Dijon mustard
Salt and pepper

How to Make It:

Add the 3 thin sliced apples into a bowl, pour over the 2 tablespoons of lemon juice, and toss to coat. Add the 3 tablespoons of extra virgin olive oil to a skillet on medium heat. Stir in the 2 cups of thin sliced onions and dashes of salt and sauté. Add the 2 tablespoons of apple cider vinegar and the 2 tablespoons of Dijon mustard in with the onions and stir with a whisk. Add the 1/4 cups of sour cream and water and continue stirring with the whisk. Pour the dressing over the lemon apples and toss. Toss in the 4 crosswise sliced endives, 2 bunches of trimmed watercress and the 1/2 pound of thin sliced and torn turkey ham. Add dashes of salt and pepper and toss before serving.

Baked Potatoes Twice

Baked potatoes are a tasty light meal, but "twice" baked potatoes are even better! Makes 4 servings.

What You'll Need:

4 potatoes (medium sized russet works best)
1/2 cup of onions (thin sliced)
1/2 cup of cream cheese with chives
1/2 cup of milk
1 tablespoon of butter
1 tablespoon of parsley (fresh chopped, plus 4 pinches)
2 teaspoons of thyme (fresh chopped)
1 teaspoon of canola oil
1 teaspoon of garlic (minced)
Salt and pepper

How to Make It:

Prep: Preheat the oven to 375 degrees Fahrenheit. Wash the potatoes, pat dry, and then rub the outside with the teaspoon of canola oil. Sprinkle salt over them and place in the oven, with a baking sheet on the rack below. Bake for 75 minutes; remove from the oven to cool.

Add the tablespoon of butter to a skillet on medium heat. Stir in the 1/2 cup of thin sliced onions and dashes of salt and pepper for about 7 minutes. Stir in the 2 teaspoons of fresh chopped thyme and the teaspoon of minced garlic, stirring for a minute. Remove from heat. Cut the potatoes in half, lengthwise, leaving the skin intact on the bottom. Carefully scoop the meat of the potato, leaving the skins intact. Place the scooped potatoes into the onion mixture and mix. Combine with the 1/2 cup of cream cheese with chives and the 1/2 cup of milk, the potatoes will be lumpy. Add the tablespoon of fresh chopped parsley and mix well. Evenly spoon the potato mixture back into the potato skins. Place the potato halves on the baking sheet and return to the hot oven for about 23 minutes. Garnish with a pinch of fresh chopped parsley and enjoy.

Broccoli Cheese Soup

Here is a lighter meal, made with wholesome broccoli, savory herbs, and delicious cheese. Makes 4 servings.

What You'll Need:

1 package of broccoli florets (frozen, 16 oz)
3 cups of chicken stock
1 1/4 cups of Cheddar cheese (shredded, sharp)
1 cup of French bread (large cubes)
1 cup of onions (sliced)
1/2 cup of heavy cream
5 tablespoons of butter (divided)
3 tablespoons of flour (all-purpose)
2 tablespoons of olive oil (extra virgin)
1/2 teaspoon of garlic (minced)
1/2 teaspoon of thyme (fresh chopped)
1/4 teaspoon of white pepper (ground)
1/4 teaspoon of Creole seasoning
Salt
Nutmeg

How to Make It:

Add 3 tablespoons of butter to a medium saucepan turn to medium high heat. Sauté the 1 cup of sliced onions and add dashes of salt, nutmeg, and 1/4 teaspoon of ground white pepper. Stir in the 1/2 teaspoon of minced garlic and the 1/2 teaspoon of fresh chopped thyme for several seconds. While stirring with a whisk, sprinkle in the 3 tablespoons of all-purpose flour, keep stirring for about 2 minutes over the heat. Pour in the 3 cups of chicken stock, continue to stir with the whisk until all the lumps are gone. Turn the heat to high to bring to a boil while stirring. Turn the heat to low and simmer for 5 minutes, stirring often. Add the 16 oz package of frozen broccoli florets and cook for another 10 minutes, stirring often. If desired, pour into a blender and food processor to blend. Or stir with a masher, mashing the broccoli. Return to the saucepan on low heat. Preheat the oven to 400 degrees Fahrenheit. Pour in the 1/2 cup of heavy cream, stirring while the cream heats. Pour in the 1 1/4 cups of Cheddar cheese, stirring until melted. Add the last 2 tablespoons of butter, stirring until melted and blended.

Put the 1 cup of large cubed French bread and toss with the 2 tablespoons of extra virgin olive oil and the 1/4 teaspoon of Creole seasoning. Spread on a baking sheet and bake for 3 minutes in the hot oven. Remove to flip the croutons over and bake another 3 minutes.

Ladle soup and top with the croutons to serve.

Cauliflower Soup

Here is a delicious and filling, yet light, soup. Makes 4 servings.

What You'll Need:

1 head of cauliflower (chopped florets)
4 parsley leaves (fresh)
6 cups of chicken stock
1 cup of potatoes (scrubbed, skin-on, cubed)
1/2 cup of milk
1/2 cup of onions (chopped)
1 tablespoon of canola oil
1 teaspoon of butter
Salt and pepper

How to Make It:

Add the tablespoon of canola oil and the teaspoon of butter to a large saucepan over medium low heat. Stir in the 1/2 cup of chopped onions, cook and stir for 10 minutes. Add the heat of chopped cauliflower florets, 6 cups of chicken stock, and the cup of cubed potatoes and season with dashes of salt and pepper. Turn the heat to high and bring liquid to a boil. Turn heat to medium, cover and cook for 20 more minutes, until the vegetables are tender. Pour the soup into a blender or food processor to combine until smooth. Pour back into the saucepan and reheat to medium. Add more salt and pepper to taste. Thick soup may be thinned with extra milk. Garnish with a fresh parsley leaf in each bowl.

Greens with Baked Beans

This is a delicious one dish meal that offers wholesome beans along with smoked turkey ham and savory herbs. Makes 6 servings.

What You'll Need:

1 bunch of greens (mustard greens or Swiss chard, chopped, stems removed)
2 cans of pinto beans (drained, rinsed, 15 oz)
1 can of navy beans (undrained, 15oz)
1 can of tomatoes (crushed 15 oz)
1/2 cup of smoked turkey ham (diced)
1/2 cup of celery (fine chopped)
1/2 cup of carrots (fine chopped)
1/4 cup of parsley (fresh chopped)
1/4 cup of onion (chopped)
1/4 cup of water
1 tablespoon of olive oil (extra virgin)
1 teaspoon of garlic (minced)
1 teaspoon of thyme (fresh chopped)
1 teaspoon of oregano (fresh chopped)
Salt and pepper

How to Make It:

Prep: Preheat oven to 375 degrees Fahrenheit. Place a large skillet on the stove on medium heat and add the tablespoon of olive oil. Stir in and sauté the 1/2 cup of celery (fine chopped), 1/2 cup of carrots (fine chopped), 1/4 cup of onion (chopped), and 1 teaspoon of garlic (minced). Season with salt and pepper. Stir in the bunch of greens along with the 1/2 cup of diced smoked turkey ham and 1/4 cup of water. Cook for 3 minutes. Stir in the can of crushed tomatoes and turn the heat to medium high for 5 minutes. Stir in the 2 cans of drained, rinsed pinto beans, and the can of undrained navy beans. Next add the 1/4 cup of parsley (fresh chopped), 1 teaspoon of thyme (fresh chopped), and the 1 teaspoon of oregano (fresh chopped). Stir and heat through. Using a potato masher, mash the some of the beans (not all). Sprinkle with salt and pepper. Pour into a baking dish (2 quart) and cover with foil. Bake for 55 minutes, removing the foil for the last 10. Allow to cool for about 5 minutes before serving.

Maple Flavored Sweet Potato Fries

Here is a healthy and sweet version of a favorite, a nice alternative to French fries. Makes 6 servings.

What You'll Need:

5 sweet potatoes (peeled and cut into small wedges)
1 tablespoon of canola oil
1 tablespoon of maple syrup
1/2 teaspoon of lemon zest
Salt and pepper
Nutmeg

How to Make It:

Prep: Preheat the oven to 425 degrees Fahrenheit. Line a baking sheet with foil.

Place the sweet potato wedges in a large bowl, add the tablespoon of canola oil, and toss to coach each piece. Add dashes of salt and pepper. Place the wedges on the foil lined baking sheet and place in the hot oven for 20 minutes. Take the baking sheet out of the oven and place the wedges back in the bowl. This time add the tablespoon of maple syrup and toss to coat all. Place the potatoes back on the baking sheet and bake for 7 minutes, then flip the potato wedges and bake another 7 minutes. Add to a serving bowl, toss with the 1/2 teaspoon of lemon zest and dashes of salt, pepper, and nutmeg before serving.

Nutty Cucumber Mango Rice Salad

Enjoy something different made with peanuts, mangos, cucumbers and rice. Makes 6 servings.

What You'll Need:

2 scallions (sliced thin)
1 cucumber (English, diced)
1 jalapeno (red, seeded, diced)
1 1/2 cups of saffron rice
1 cup of mango (chopped)
1/2 cup of cilantro (fresh chopped)
1/3 cup of peanuts (salted, roasted, chopped)
1/4 cup of quinoa (rinsed)
2 tablespoons of lime juice
2 tablespoons of canola oil
1 tablespoon of lime zest
1 teaspoon of sugar (granulated)
Salt and pepper
Water

How to Make It:

Cook the 1 1/2 cups of saffron rice according to the package directions. In another saucepan add water and dashes of water and turn heat to high to bring to a boil.

Stir in the 1/4 cup of rinsed quinoa and turn heat to medium high. Cook for 12 minutes, until it turns tender. Pour into a colander and rinse with cool water and drain. In a separate bowl, combine the 2 tablespoons of lime juice, 2 tablespoons of canola oil, tablespoon of lime zest, teaspoon of granulated sugar and dashes of salt and pepper, using a whisk. Stir in the cook saffron rice, 2 thin sliced scallions, diced English cucumber, seeded and diced red jalapeno, cup of chopped mango, 1/2 cup of fresh chopped cilantro 1/3 cup of salted, roasted, chopped peanuts, and the cooked quinoa. Toss and season with more salt and pepper if desired.

Open Face Tomato and Mozzarella Herb Sandwich

This is a unique twist from a sandwich; there is no meat, just the delicious tomato and smoked Mozzarella with savory herbs on a baguette roll.   Makes 4 servings.

What You'll Need:

4 slices of smoked mozzarella (thick)
4 slices of tomato (thick)
1 demi baguette (4 oz.)
2 tablespoons of parsley (fresh chopped)
1 1/2 tablespoons of Parmesan cheese (fine grated)
2 teaspoons of thyme (fresh chopped)
2 teaspoons of olive oil
1 teaspoon of garlic (minced)
Salt and pepper

How to Make It:

Prep: Preheat the oven to broil.

In a bowl, add the 2 tablespoons of fresh chopped parsley, 2 teaspoons of fresh chopped thyme, teaspoon of minced garlic and 2 teaspoons of olive oil and combine. Slice the baguette lengthwise in two. Cut in half so you have 4 pieces of bread. Evenly divide and spread the herbs over the bread, face up. Evenly sprinkle the 1 1/2 tablespoons of fine grated Parmesan cheese over the 4 slices. Bake under the broiler for 2 minutes. Remove and add a slice of tomato, and a slice of smoked mozzarella cheese on top of each slice of bread. Return to the broiler long enough for the cheese to melt, about a minute or two. Serve hot.

Orange Stir Fry Vegetables

This is a light dish made with just vegetables with the light fruity flavor of orange. Makes 4 servings.

What You'll Need:

1 can of water chestnuts (drained, 4oz)
1 cup of orange juice
1 cup of celery (chopped)
1 cup of mushrooms (rinsed, sliced)
1/2 cup of bell pepper (red, thin sliced)
1/2 cup of carrots (sliced)
1/2 cup of squash (sliced yellow)
1/2 cup of broccoli (chopped)
1/4 cup of baby corn
1/4 cup of snow peas
1/8 cup of onions (thin sliced)
2 tablespoons of cornstarch
2 tablespoons of orange zest
2 tablespoons of canola oil (divided)
1 tablespoon of soy sauce
1 teaspoon of ginger (chopped)
1 teaspoon of garlic (minced)
Salt
4 orange slices
Cooked rice (enough for 4 servings)

How to Make It:

Pour the cup of orange juice into a bowl and combine with the 2 tablespoons of cornstarch, tablespoon of soy sauce, teaspoon of chopped ginger, teaspoon of minced garlic and dashes of salt. Add a wok or large skillet to high heat and pour in the tablespoon of canola oil and sauté the cup of sliced mushrooms, 1/2 cup of sliced carrots, and the 1/8 cup of thin sliced onions for just one minute. Mix in the 1/2 cup of sliced yellow squash, 1/2 cup of chopped broccoli, and 1/4 cup of snow peas. Stir in the 4 oz can of drained water chestnuts, cup of chopped celery, 1/2 cup of thin sliced red bell peppers, and 1/4 cup of baby corn. Cook for another couple of minutes. Pour in the orange sauce, stir and heat through. Serve over the cooked rice and garnish with the 2 tablespoons of orange zest and an orange slice on each plate.

Parsley Mint Roasted Carrots

This is a delicious way to eat your carrots, and nutritious to boot. Makes 4 servings.

What You'll Need:

2 1/2 cups of carrots (halved lengthwise and cut into 2-inch chunks)
1/2 cup of chicken stock
1/4 cup of mint (fresh chopped)
1/4 cup of parsley (fresh chopped)
4 teaspoons of olive oil
2 teaspoons of lemon juice
1/2 teaspoon of lemon zest
Salt and pepper

How to Make It:

Pour the 1/2 cup of chicken broth in a skillet and turn to medium high heat. Add the 2/12 cups of chunked carrots and a teaspoon of olive oil, stir, and bring to a boil. Place a lid on, reduce heat to medium, and cook for 13 more minutes. Remove the lid, stir and cook off all of the chicken stock and cook the carrots another 3 minutes to slight brown. Add dashes of salt and pepper. In a small bowl mix the 1/4 cup of fresh chopped mint,

1/4 cup of fresh chopped parsley, 2 teaspoons of lemon juice and 1/2 teaspoon of lemon zest. Place the carrots in a serving bowl and toss with the mint, parsley mixture. Serve warm.

Quinoa with Herbs

Quinoa is a super food because of the high levels of nutrients within it. Makes 4 servings.

What You'll Need:

2 3/4 cups of chicken stock
1 1/2 cups of quinoa
3/4 cup of basil (fresh chopped leaves)
1/4 cup of parsley (fresh chopped)
1/2 cup of lemon juice (divided)
1/4 cup of olive oil (extra virgin)
1 tablespoon of thyme (fresh chopped leaves)
2 teaspoons of lemon zest
Salt and pepper

How to Make It:

Pour the 2 3/4 cups of chicken stock into a medium size saucepan along with the 1 1/2 cups of quinoa and the 1/4 cup of lemon juice, turn to medium high heat, and bring to a boil. Place lid on saucepan, turn to low, and simmer for about 14 minutes. Meanwhile, combine the 3/4 cup of basil (fresh chopped leaves), 1/4 cup of parsley (fresh chopped), 1/4 cup of lemon juice (divided), 1/4 cup of olive oil (extra virgin), 1 tablespoon of thyme (fresh chopped leaves), 2 teaspoons of lemon zest, and dashes of salt and pepper in a small bowl. When the quinoa is cooked, add to a serving bowl and pour the "dressing" over, tossing to coat all. Add extra salt and pepper if desired.

Spicy Tomatoes and Green Beans

Sometimes you just need a pick-me-up and this dish will do it with the light flavor of cinnamon with tomatoes and green beans. Makes 6 servings.

What You'll Need:

4 cups of green beans (trimmed)
1 can of tomatoes (15 oz crushed)
1 1/4 cups of water
1/4 cup of onions (chopped)
3 tablespoons of olive oil
Salt and pepper
Cinnamon

How to Make It:

Add the 3 tablespoons to a skillet and sauté the 1/4 cup of onions. In a medium saucepan, add the 4 cups of green beans (trimmed), 1 can of tomatoes (15 oz crushed), 1 1/4 cups of water, sautéed onions, and dashes of salt and pepper and cinnamon. Stir and bring the water to a boil over high heat. Turn to medium low and simmer partial cover with a lid on for 35 minutes or until the green beans is tender. Season with more salt and pepper if desired.

Spinach Salad with Pomegranate Dressing

Spinach salad is a delicious meal made with pomegranate juice and walnuts, guaranteed to delight the taste buds. Makes 4 servings.

What You'll Need:

4 cups of spinach (baby)
1 cup of mushrooms (white button, sliced thin)
3/4 cup of tomatoes (grape, halved)
1/2 cup of walnuts (chopped)
1/4 cup of onions (thin sliced)
1/4 cup of pomegranate juice (plus 2 tablespoons)
1 tablespoon of apple cider vinegar
1 tablespoon of olive oil (extra virgin)
1 teaspoon of sugar (granulated)
Salt and pepper
Water and ice

How to Make It:

Pour 1/4 cup of pomegranate juice into a skillet and add the teaspoon of granulated sugar and a couple of dashes of salt. Turn heat to medium high and simmer for several minutes, stir often. Stir in the 1/2 cup of chopped walnuts and cook for another 5 minutes, the liquid should evaporate. Pour the nuts onto a cool baking sheet break apart when cooled.

Place the 1/4 cup of thin sliced onions in a bowl and cover with ice and water for 10 minutes. Drain the water and dry the onions with a paper towel. Put the 4 cups of baby spinach in a salad bowl, and then layer the cold onions, followed by the cup of thin sliced white button mushrooms, 3/4 cup of halved grape tomatoes, and the walnuts. In a separate bowl, combine the 2 tablespoons of pomegranate juice with the tablespoon of apple cider vinegar, tablespoon of extra virgin olive oil, and dashes of salt and pepper, using a whisk. Pour the dressing over the spinach salad and toss, and then serve.

www.ingramcontent.com/pod-product-compliance
Ingram Content Group UK Ltd.
Pitfield, Milton Keynes, MK11 3LW, UK
UKHW022227230426
12048UKWH00016BA/1106